ANNIHIL

screenplay by
ALEX GARLAND

based on the novel by
JEFF VANDERMEER

FABER & FABER

First published in 2018
by Faber & Faber Limited
Bloomsbury House
74–77 Great Russell Street
London WC1B 3DA

First published in the USA in 2018

Typeset by Country Setting, Kingsdown, Kent CT14 8ES
Printed annd bound by CPI Group (UK) Ltd, Croydon CR0 4YY

Photographs © Miya Mizuno

The right of Alex Garland to be identified
as author of this work has been asserted in accordance with
Section 77 of the Copyright, Designs and Patents Act 1988

A CIP record for this book is available from the British Library

ISBN 978–0–571–34615–8

2 4 6 8 10 9 7 5 3 1

Annihilation

THE SCREENPLAY

Open on:

INT. INTERROGATION ROOM

Lena is seated in the interrogation room.

Lomax and two scientists are standing. Facing her.

Behind glass, more scientists observe.

A beat, before Lomax speaks.

> LOMAX
>
> What did you eat?

> LENA
>
> . . . I don't remember eating.

> LOMAX
>
> You were inside for nearly four months. You had rations for two weeks. You must have eaten something.

Lena pauses.

> LENA
>
> I suppose time refracted along with everything else. Josie would have appreciated that. I think she was the one who understood it best.

> LOMAX
>
> Josie Radek?

> LENA
>
> Yes.

> LOMAX
>
> What happened to Josie Radek?

Lena pauses.

LENA

I don't know.

LOMAX

What happened to Ventress? Sheppard? Thorensen?

LENA

I don't know. Dead, or . . .

LOMAX

Or?

Lena shrugs. Not obstructive. Helpless.

LENA

I don't know.

Silence.

LOMAX

What do you know?

EXT. OUTER ATMOSPHERE – NIGHT

A meteor burns in the outer atmosphere. It races towards the planet.

EXT. LIGHTHOUSE

Blaze as it hits the ground by the lighthouse, lighting up like phosphorous . . .

. . . and drills into the earth.

Cut to:

An utterly alien form.

It has tendrils. It shimmers with iridescent colour. It has immense fractal complexity in its shape. And it's moving. Gently, like a sea anemone in a swell.

ANNIHILATION

A cell, through a microscope lens.

Then we hear a woman's voice.

WOMAN
(out of shot)

This is a cell.

As we watch, the cell starts to divide.

Like all cells, it is born from an existing cell.

The creature is now halfway through the division, separating into a mirror of itself.

By extension, all cells were ultimately born from one cell. A single organism, alone on planet Earth, perhaps alone in the universe, about four billion years ago.

The creature completes its division –

And immediately its two halves start the same process again.

One became two. Two became four. Then eight. Sixteen. Thirty-two. The rhythm of the dividing pair, which becomes the structure of every microbe, blade of grass, sea creature, land creature, and human. The structure of everything that lives –

Cut to:

INT. JOHNS HOPKINS MEDICAL SCHOOL/SEMINAR ROOM – DAY

Professor Lena Kerans:

Thirty-one years old. Recently completed her doctorate, now teaching a seminar class of first-year medical students.

LENA

– and everything that dies.

Beat.

5

As students of medicine, as the doctors of tomorrow, that's where you come in.

She gestures to the screen behind her – which shows the electron microscope images that we have been watching.

The cell you've been looking at is from a tumour. Female patient, early thirties, taken from her cervix. Over the course of the coming term . . .

Lena pauses.

A couple of the med students look up from their note-taking, aware of the silence –

And see that their tutor has been momentarily distracted.

Her head is turned to the window, where outside, above the treetops, a full moon hangs in the blue sky.

The image of the moon in daylight is gently surreal. Arresting, because the sky is so cloudless and clear.

Absently, Lena's hand goes to her neck, and her fingers lightly touch a silver locket that hangs from a slender chain.

As the silence extends, the students exchange a glance.

Then Lena becomes aware she has zoned out.

She picks up the thread.

LENA

Over the course of the coming term, we will be closely examining these cancer cells in vitro, and observing autophagic activity.

INT. JOHNS HOPKINS MEDICAL SCHOOL/CAMPUS – DAY

Lena walks through the campus, joined as she walks by one of the faces from her seminar: Katie, an earnest young med student.

LENA

Hey, Katie.

KATIE

I read the John Sulston paper last night.

LENA

You're working too hard, Katie.

KATIE

I keep feeling I'm not working hard enough. Like I'm behind the other students. I think they find everything easier.

Their exchange is watched by a man in his mid-forties, waiting ahead. Daniel Maitland.

LENA

You aren't. And they don't.

KATIE

I'll read it again this evening anyway.

LENA

Katie, it's a Friday night. You're at college. Go out. Have fun. Or I'll fail you this quarter.

Katie smiles.

KATIE

. . . Okay.

Lena notices Daniel.

Katie peels off.

Daniel smiles in greeting.

DANIEL

Lena.

LENA

Dan.

Lena doesn't break stride, so Daniel falls in step beside her.

DANIEL

I keep looking for you at lunch, but you never seem to be around.

7

LENA

I've been catching up on some writing.

DANIEL

All work and no play. It's not healthy.

Lena keeps walking.

I wanted to ask. Do you have plans Saturday?

LENA

. . . Saturday.

DANIEL

Sarah and I have a few people coming over. A garden party, while the weather holds.

Lena gives the neutral frown of someone prepping a polite excuse.

LENA

You mean tomorrow?

DANIEL

Yes.

LENA

Actually, I do have something planned.

DANIEL

Are you sure? I think it'll be a lot of fun. We've asked Amir and Jenny, and –

LENA

(*cuts in*)

Thanks, Dan. I appreciate it. But I was going to paint our bedroom.

Lena corrects herself immediately.

The bedroom.

Daniel looks at Lena.

DANIEL

It's been a year, Lena. You're allowed to come to a barbecue.

He reaches out, and catches Lena's arm.

It's not a betrayal. Not an insult to his memory.

Beat.

> LENA

I'm going to paint the bedroom.

Daniel gives way. Removes his hand.

> DANIEL

Home improvements.

Lena smiles perfunctorily.

> LENA

Yes.

EXT. SUBURB – DAY

Bright, flat sunlight pushes through tree tops.

A broad road. Detached houses. Green lawns. Two children on pushbikes glide down the sidewalk.

INT. HOUSE – CONTINUOUS

A quiet house, with stillness in the rooms.

Photographs in the bedroom show a couple: Lena, with a man in his early thirties, Kane.

One of these images show both Kane and Lena in military uniform, in a baked landscape of rock and dust.

Kane smiles easily at the camera. Full of life in these frozen snapshots.

Another of the images shows a wedding. Lena in white. The couple embracing.

INT. HOUSE/LIVING ROOM – CONTINUOUS

Lena sits on the sofa, legs curled beneath her.

In one hand, she holds her silver locket.

It's open. Inside is a photo of Kane.

She gazes at it.

We can feel Lena's effort to modulate her breathing. Inhaling and exhaling through parted lips.

Less controlled, tears spill down her face. Down her cheeks and neck. Into the corner of her mouth.

Title:

ANNIHILATION

Then, into the quiet and stillness, Music intrudes.

Cut to:

INT. HOUSE/BEDROOM – DAY

The speakers from which the music is playing.

The framed photographs of Lena and Kane, which are now off the walls, and stacked on the landing.

A plastic sheet as it rises up, billows, then settles over the double bed.

A flathead screwdriver pushes under the rim of a tub of paint and pops the lid.

Lena runs a primed roller over the wall. Leaving a fat white stripe over the old colour. Flecking her shirt and face with paint. Smearing it off her forehead with the back of her hand.

Repainting the room is an act of moving on.

She is energised. So focused –

– that she doesn't see the figure that appears in the doorway of the bedroom.

Kane.

He seems different to the photos. In uniform, but bloodless in his complexion. Clean-shaven. Neat hair.

He watches Lena painting. Oddly blank. Not announcing his presence –

– until she turns, needing to reload the roller –

– and sees him.

First, she jolts at the sight of the figure.

Second, she recognises him.

LENA
(whispers)

Oh God.

The roller slips from her hand.

Lands with a wet slap on the floor.

She walks towards Kane.

Puts a hand on his cheek, in the way she might touch a clear window to see if it holds a pane of glass.

Then she grabs his face with both palms. Kissing him as she talks.

LENA

Oh God, oh God – I thought you were gone – gone forever – forever.

She's crying, laughing.

He isn't.

Her passion is completely unmatched by his. He is glazed and distant. No more than compliant.

Until finally she has to acknowledge it.

She breaks off. Hurt, confused.

And as she breaks off, he then leans forward, not apparently reading her expression, and kisses her once on the lips.

It feels wrong. Emphasises the strangeness.

> LENA
> . . . Kane?

INT. HOUSE/KITCHEN – NIGHT

Kane sits at the table.

In front of him is a glass of water. He stares at the clear liquid, but doesn't drink it.

Lena stands by the counter. Her confusion has transformed now into frustration and anger.

> LENA
> You must be able to tell me something. Vanished off the face of the Earth for twelve months! I deserve a better explanation than no explanation.

Kane doesn't answer.

> No one knew anything about your unit. I contacted everyone. Everyone I could. The other wives and partners knew as little as me.

Beat.

> Was it covert?

> KANE
> . . . Maybe.

> LENA
> What does that mean: 'maybe'?

> KANE
> Okay, yes. Covert. I think so.

> LENA
> Pakistan again.

Beat.

> Yemen?

                                KANE

I can't tell you.

                                LENA

So it is classified.

                                KANE

I don't know. Where it was. Or what it was.

                                LENA

How can that even be possible? Was it hot? Was there
snow? Did the people speak Swahili, or Portuguese, or
Pashto?

Kane says nothing.

*Lena processes. Fighting back the strangeness of the conversation.
Trying to assert reason.*

                                LENA

How long have you been back?

                                KANE

I don't know.

                                LENA

Well – how did you get back? Which base did they fly
you to?

                                KANE

I don't know.

                                LENA

What about the rest of your unit? Did they return with
you?

*For the first time, we see something tangible in Kane.
A helplessness. A dimly understood fear.*

                                KANE

Does it matter?

Silence.

*As Lena suddenly understands: her husband is profoundly
damaged. His body has returned to her, but not his mind.*

She takes a seat opposite him at the table.

Then takes his hand. He doesn't resist.

> LENA

Kane.

He looks at her.

> LENA

How did you get home?

> KANE

I –

He breaks off a moment.

I was outside.

> LENA

Outside the house.

> KANE

No. Outside the room. The room with a bed. The door was open, and I saw you. I remembered you. Your face.

Silence.

Then Kane detaches his hand from Lena's.

He reaches for the glass of water. Takes a single sip. Then puts the glass back down.

Reveal: in the water, a strand of blood hangs. Suspended.

It can only be from inside Kane's mouth.

Kane looks up at Lena.

I don't think I'm very well.

Cut to:

INT. AMBULANCE – NIGHT

The interior of an ambulance, driving fast through the night streets. Siren howling.

Kane – strapped to a stretcher in the back, rolled-back eyes, half raised – coughs blood.

A Paramedic tries to support him with one arm while speaking urgently into a radio.

PARAMEDIC
Male, thirty-one, haemorrhage, in seizure.

Kneeling by Kane, Lena wipes at the blood on his face. Tries to hold his lolling head.

LENA
Baby, baby, stay with me –

PARAMEDIC
Prepare emergency team for ETA in six minutes –

Suddenly the Paramedic is interrupted by a second siren joining the first. Then a third and fourth.

Blue lights start pulsing through the windows.

The Paramedic shouts to the Ambulance Driver.

You call for a police escort?

AMBULANCE DRIVER
They aren't police!

PARAMEDIC
What the hell?

The Paramedic looks out of the window, and as he does so –

The interior of the ambulance is flooded with blinding white light and a roar of engine noise.

From Lena's bleached face, disorientated by the horror and sensory overload. Cut to:

EXT. STREET – CONTINUOUS

The street outside the ambulance, where the reason for the noise and light is explained.

The ambulance is flanked by three black SUVs, and above it a helicopter, metres off the ground. Shining a spotlight straight down at the front windscreen.

Cut to:

INT. AMBULANCE – CONTINUOUS

The Ambulance Driver –

AMBULANCE DRIVER

Jesus!

– dazzled, slamming his foot on the brakes –

EXT. STREET – CONTINUOUS

– sending the vehicle into a skid –

INT. AMBULANCE – CONTINUOUS

– which slams Lena and the Paramedic hard against the wall of the vehicle.

The semi-conscious Kane is held fast by the stretcher straps.

EXT. STREET – CONTINUOUS

The ambulance skids to a stop, and the SUVs expertly slide to halt around it.

They immediately disgorge uniformed armed men. Black gear, stubby semi-automatic machine guns. Spec Ops.

The Spec Ops soldiers pull open the rear doors of the ambulance.

Drag out Lena and the Paramedic.

Above, the helicopter hovers. Obscuring our vision, and deafening us.

Through the obliterating rotor-blade wash, we can hear Lena.

LENA
(*screaming*)
What are you doing? Let him go! Let him go!

Cut to:

Lena, fighting as two of the Spec Ops try to hold her.

The Paramedic and Driver being dragged out of view.

Kane pulled on his stretcher from the ambulance.

Something jammed into Lena's neck. A one-hit disposable syringe.

The tranquilliser drops to the floor, as the fight bleeds out of Lena. Then consciousness.

Black screen.

Caption:

PART ONE – SOUTHERN REACH

Cut to:

INT. HOUSE/LIVING ROOM – NIGHT

Lena and Kane, on the sofa.

Lena is sitting at one end.

Kane is sprawled at the other.

Lena has a book in her hands, but is not reading. She's gazing into middle distance.

Kane is watching her not reading.

Beats pass.

KANE
Hey.

There is a delay before Lena reacts.

Then her head turns to him.

17

She smiles slightly distantly.

LENA

. . . Hey.

Cut to:

INT. SOUTHERN REACH FACILITY/INTERVIEW ROOM

Lena. Sleeping.

She's been cleaned up. She's been changed out of her bloodstained clothes into an orange jumpsuit.

She stirs. Wakes. Opens her eyes.

Reacts.

Reveal: Lena is in a cell-like room.

There is the bed, on which she lies. There is a single chair. There is a steel sink, attached to the wall.

And opposite there is a glass door, through which there is what looks like a corridor – and an armed Spec Ops Guard, watching her.

Seeing that Lena is awake, the Spec Ops Guard turns and speaks to someone out of sight. Inaudible to us, through the soundproof glass.

A moment later, that person appears.

A woman in her early fifties. Glasses. Suit. Holding a small plastic bottle of mineral water:

Dr Ventress.

Lena sits up on the bed.

The two women observe each other for a beat through the glass.

Lena trembling slightly. Adrenaline jamming the drugged sleep out of her mind.

Then Dr Ventress unlocks the door. The sudden noise startles Lena.

A beat.

DR VENTRESS

Hello.

The doctor enters the room and closes the door – which locks behind her.

I imagine you feel dreadful. It's the hangover from the sedative you were given. Queasy. Nasty metal taste in the mouth.

Lena looks at her.

Would you like some water?

The doctor holds out the plastic bottle.

Lena hesitates.

Then, with slightly uncertain fingers, takes it.

Returns the woman's gaze.

LENA

Who are you?

DR VENTRESS

My name is Dr Ventress. I'm a psychologist.

LENA

Why am I talking to a psychologist?

Dr Ventress ignores the question. She takes the chair opposite Lena, and sits down.

LENA

Am I in a psychiatric hospital?

DR VENTRESS

No.

LENA

Then what? Where am I? And where's my husband?

Again, Dr Ventress ignores the question.

                    DR VENTRESS

You're a biologist.

                        LENA

So what?

                    DR VENTRESS

You served in the military for seven years before returning
to education. You completed a doctorate at Johns Hopkins.
Your research area was the genetically programmed life
cycle of the cell.

Lena leans forwards. Enunciates.

                        LENA

Where is my husband?

                    DR VENTRESS

Yes. I'd like to talk about Sergeant Kane. When did he
arrive home?

                        LENA

That depends on how long I've been here.

Dr Ventress gives nothing.

                    DR VENTRESS

Did he explain how he reached your house?

                        LENA

No.

                    DR VENTRESS

Had he contacted you at any point over the last few
months?

                        LENA

No. He left on – whatever he was doing. Whatever spec-
ops mission. That was the last I heard until he reappeared.

                    DR VENTRESS

What did he tell you about the mission he had been on?

                        LENA

Nothing.

DR VENTRESS

What about before he left? Did he ever mention what he was doing, or where he was going?

LENA

He never said. I never asked.

DR VENTRESS

But you made regular requests for information about him to his unit CO until six months ago. Then you stopped. Why was that?

Lena takes a breath.

LENA

Because we had an agreement. Between us. Six months of radio silence meant I was to assume he was dead. And move on.

DR VENTRESS

It's not easy to move on.

LENA

I didn't.

Silence.

LENA

You're CIA.

Lena sits back in her chair.

LENA

You're CIA. And Kane was on some kind of covert operation for you.

No reaction.

I think I'm done answering questions. It's your turn.

Beat.

DR VENTRESS

Your husband is in the same building as you. And I should tell you, he's extremely ill.

LENA

Ill in what way?

DR VENTRESS

We don't actually know. He doesn't test positive for any
known condition. But objectively, his body is haemorrhaging
and his organs are failing.

LENA

He's dying.

DR VENTRESS

Yes.

Lena swallows. Stays composed.

LENA

Those symptoms. He must have been exposed to
something. Radiation. A virus of some sort.

Dr Ventress adds nothing.

You have to tell me where he's been and what was he
doing. I might actually be able to help him.

DR VENTRESS

I can't talk about that. You understand.

LENA

Clearly, I don't!

DR VENTRESS

You understand that I'm not going to talk about it.

The doctor stands.

*Outside the cell, the Spec Ops Guard unlocks the door in
anticipation of her exit.*

I'll be back later.

LENA

You still haven't told me anything about what's going on
or what I'm doing here!

Dr Ventress has reached the door.

We'll speak again.

The door closes. Locks.

Cut to:

INT. SOUTHERN REACH FACILITY/CORRIDOR

The Spec Ops Guard. And his view of Lena.

Cut to:

INT. SOUTHERN REACH FACILITY/INTERVIEW ROOM

Lena.

Washing her face in the sink.

Trying to get clarity into her mind.

She lifts her face.

Above the sink there is a small mirror.

In it she sees the confines of what is clearly her cell.

The red mark on her neck from where she was injected.

Her fingers go to it for a moment.

She closes her eyes.

Breathes.

Opens her eyes. Meets her own gaze.

                    LENA
                    (quiet)
      No.

Cut to:

INT. SOUTHERN REACH FACILITY/CORRIDOR

The Spec Ops Guard, watching as Lena approaches the glass.

She looks directly at the Guard. Her gaze flicks momentarily to his belt. Then back to his face.

Then she speaks. Then knocks on the glass.

He hears nothing.

He taps a comms button on an earpiece.

Talks into a radio.

> SPEC OPS GUARD
> She wants something.

Beat.

> Copy.

The Spec Ops Guard reaches forward.

Unlocks the door.

It slides open.

> If you require food or water, or are feeling nauseous, we can attend to that.

Lena takes a half-step forwards.

> LENA
> I just want to know if you can tell me anything about my husband.

> SPEC OPS GUARD
> Stop there, please, ma'am.

> LENA
> I just need to know what's happened to him.

> SPEC OPS GUARD
> Step back into the room, ma'am.

But rather than take a step back, she takes another step forward, towards the soldier.

Her eyes brim.

                          LENA
    Please.

                    SPEC OPS GUARD
    Ma'am.

A tear spills.

Her hand touches the soldier's arm.

                          LENA
    If you know anything at all, can't you just –

It's a ploy.

*With her other hand, Lena has reached to his belt – which holds
a clip containing two of the one-hit syringe vials that were used
to sedate her.*

*In a moment, it's unclipped, up, and jammed into the soldier's
neck.*

                    SPEC OPS GUARD
    Ah! Bitch –

His hand claws at the vial. Knocks it out.

All too late. He exhales. Folds. Falls.

*Lena stares at him, as if trying to absorb and comprehend what
she has just done.*

Then she reaches down. Takes the man's handgun.

*Lena can now go left or right. Each direction is blocked by a
ward door. But to the left, a Nurse can be seen through a glass
panel in the door, in conversation with someone out of sight.*

She heads right.

INT. SOUTHERN REACH FACILITY/CORRIDOR –
CONTINUOUS

*Lena runs through the facility. Padding on the linoleum floor in
her white sneakers.*

Cut to:

INT. SOUTHERN REACH FACILITY/SECURITY DOOR –
CONTINUOUS

A yellow frosted-glass security door.

On the door, a sign reads:

WARNING! YOU ARE LEAVING THE QUARANTINE AREA
NO EXIT WITHOUT CLEARANCE

Lena attempts to push it. Pull it.

Inevitably, it's locked.

*A frozen beat: Lena, hyperventilating slightly in the silent
corridor. Staring at the frosted security door, with the Spec Ops
Guard's sidearm in her hand.*

                         LENA
   Oh shit. Oh shit.

*She suddenly lifts the gun and fires at the middle of the glass
door.*

The noise is deafening. The glass collapses.

A moment later, an alarm starts to sound.

INT. SOUTHERN REACH FACILITY/LOBBY – CONTINUOUS

Outside the quarantine area is a lobby with an elevator.

Lena enters the elevator –

INT. SOUTHERN REACH FACILITY/ELEVATOR –
CONTINUOUS

*– and once inside, hurriedly scans for a control panel, but there
is nothing. No buttons, no input device. Just a glass panel on
one wall, with an outline of a hand etched onto the surface.*

A biometric palm reader.

She touches the pad.

An error code sounds –

LENA

Come on, please.

– and the elevator door closes, muffling the sound of the alarm.

No, no, no . . .

A terrible sense that she has managed to escape from a small locked room into an even smaller one.

Then suddenly –

– the elevator starts moving.

Upwards.

Lena waits, trying to stay calm.

Wipes sweat off her forehead.

Positions herself against the side of the car, knowing that someone must have called the elevator, and will find her inside.

Then –

– there is a slight lurch as the elevator stops.

Lena holds her handgun behind her back.

And a beat later, the doors open –

– revealing a man in a white lab coat. A Scientist of some sort. His head is dropped, reading through a sheaf of forms.

He steps inside, not looking up to Lena.

SCIENTIST

Hey.

Lena gulps back her fear. Controls her voice.

LENA

. . . Hey.

Lena can either stay or go.

Outside the lift doors, there seems to be daylight.

She makes a snap decision, and exits just as the doors start to close.

The movement makes the Scientist look up, and he glimpses Lena, in her bright orange jumpsuit.

From his puzzled expression, cut to:

INT. SOUTHERN REACH FACILITY/OBSERVATION AREA – CONTINUOUS

The elevator doors closing behind Lena.

The daylight that silhouettes her is bright, burnished, gold. As if the sun is low in the sky, and shining directly to her.

Half blinded, Lena can hear noise. People and activity; a hum of electronics; tapped keyboards; quiet conversation.

For a moment, Lena hesitates.

Then she steps forwards –

– into a large space.

It's as long as a train platform.

One wall is missing. No glass, no concrete, open to the elements.

Along the entire length of the room is an array of strange machinery. Objects that look like satellite dishes, and radio masts, and telescopes. Around them, less interpretable shapes. Industrial lasers, turbines, and glittering screens of fine gold mesh, hanging like sails.

And all the objects are oriented in one direction: towards the missing wall. Towards the light.

Lena stops again.

There's something strange about the sunlight. It's moving. Dancing slightly.

On the wall behind Lena, it casts ripples of brightness, like sun reflecting off water.

Around her, Scientists work the machines. Men and women in lab coats.

One, nearby, sees her. Rises, challenging her.

SCIENTIST

Who are you?

He tries to block her path.

She lifts an arm, revealing her gun.

LENA

Get out of my way!

Panicked, he sidesteps, jumping out of Lena's path.

Lena starts to run.

SCIENTIST
(yells)

Security! Over here!

Ahead of Lena, further down the room, Spec Ops Soldiers appear.

SPEC OPS SOLDIER 1
(into radio)

We've got her – she's on the observation deck.

SCIENTIST 2

You! Stop!

Lena ducks between machinery.

She went down there!

Knocks directly into a female scientist. Sends them both crashing to the floor.

Someone else tries to catch her arm.

Lena pulls away from them.

More Spec Ops appear from the other end of the space.

Lena has nowhere to go except into the sunlight.

EXT. SOUTHERN REACH FACILITY/VIEWING PLATFORM –
DAY

Lena manages only five or six steps into the brightness.

Then stops.

Partly because she has run out of road. But also because she has been arrested by the sight in front of her.

First reveal that Lena is standing on a viewing platform. Essentially a massive balcony, three storeys above the ground.

And the facility from which she has emerged turns out to be a kind of gatehouse structure – like a medieval castle, dragged into a brutalist twenty-first century.

Either side of the facility, a concrete wall extends. Massive, buttressed, punctuated with watch towers. It looks designed to contain or defend against something mythic in scale.

This would be a stunning sight in its own right – but it's the view from the platform that stopped Lena in her tracks.

Now reveal the landscape, behind which the sun sets.

A stretch of bare ground, for a few hundred yards beyond the concrete wall, leading to a dense forest.

And in front of – or permeating – the forest, there is a shimmer.

Similar to a heat haze – it gives a glassy liquid quality to everything seen through its prism.

But unlike a heat haze – and like a prism – it splits light.

So, through the shimmer –

– the sun distorts into a deliquescing orange orb, fringed with chromatic aberrations of blue and green.

– the colours on the clouds split into a full rainbow spectrum, spread across the sky like psychedelic Northern Lights.

– the trees in the forest distort gently, as if pushed by a gentle wind that eases the trunks into movement, as if they were as light as leaves.

DR VENTRESS

I can imagine how confusing this is to you.

Lena turns at the sound of Dr Ventress's voice.

She sees the older woman standing behind her, and a man in his early forties: Lomax, the chief of Southern Reach.

Behind them is an arc of three Spec Ops Soldiers, pointing their guns at Lena's head.

Dr Ventress takes a step towards Lena.

SPEC OPS SOLDIER 2

Sir!

Dr Ventress waves the man quiet.

DR VENTRESS

You must feel as if you're in a dream.

Lena stares back at Dr Ventress.

LENA

. . . Am I?

DR VENTRESS

No.

Dr Ventress takes another step towards Lena.

May we focus on the immediate? I don't want this moment to unravel. Would you please drop the gun?

A beat.

Lena.

Lena looks back at the melting landscape.

Then, as if letting herself be overwhelmed by the strangeness of it all, she lets the sidearm slip from her hand.

The Spec Ops immediately rush her. One kicks her pistol away, while another forces her to the ground.

Dr Ventress turns to Lomax.

Lomax gazes down at Lena dispassionately. Considering.

> LOMAX
>
> What do you think she knows?

> DR VENTRESS
>
> Nothing.

> LOMAX
>
> But she's seen it now. Can't see us letting her leave.

> DR VENTRESS
>
> . . . No.

Then gives a slight nod.

> LOMAX
>
> Might as well get her up to speed.

EXT. THE SHIMMER/TREELINE – DUSK

Sequenced images of the shimmering treeline.

> DR VENTRESS
> (*out of shot*)
>
> A religious event.

The images rotate through different filters.

> An extra-terrestrial event.

Long-lens, infra-red, thermo, solarised.

> A higher dimension.

INT. SOUTHERN REACH FACILITY/VENTRESS OFFICE –
CONTINUOUS

Reveal: we are with Lena, watching the filtered images on a monitor in the office of Dr Ventress.

> DR VENTRESS
>
> We have many theories. And very few facts.

Dr Ventress stands behind Lena.

Behind Ventress is a landscape window, looking over the deforested area towards the forest.

It started around three years ago. Blackwater National Park reported that a lighthouse on the coast was surrounded by something they termed a 'shimmer'. One of the wardens entered to investigate. Never returned.

INT. MONITOR SCREEN – CONTINUOUS

On the monitor screen we see a silent feed from a helmet cam: a continuous first-person point-of-view, showing a group of seven men and women walking across an open area of ground, towards the boundary of the Shimmer.

DR VENTRESS
The event was immediately classified. Appropriate government agencies and allies were informed.

Three of the group are soldiers, and armed. The rest appear to be scientists, carrying scanning equipment. Their faces show a mixture of fear and excitement.

DR VENTRESS
(*out of shot*)
Since then, we've sent in drones, animals, radio-waves, particle-streams –

As the group enter the boundary point of the Shimmer, the image starts to digitise and fall apart.

– and teams of people.

Then the distortions become unrecognisable.

But nothing comes back. Crossing the boundary is a one-way trip.

INT. SOUTHERN REACH FACILITY/VENTRESS OFFICE – CONTINUOUS

Pure abstraction on the monitor screen.

DR VENTRESS

Moreover, the boundary is expanding. Three metres a day. So far, eating into barely populated swampland, which we evacuated on the pretext of a chemical spill. But that won't stand much longer. In a few months, the area will have reached where we are right now. After that, we're talking about cities, and states . . .

Lena gazes at the static. Absorbed.

. . . and so on.

The monitor flicks back to a view of the Shimmer.

You okay?

Lena processes a beat. Then turns.

LENA

One question.

Beat.

LENA

You said nothing comes back. But something has.

DR VENTRESS

. . . Yes.

LENA

Will you let me see him?

INT. SOUTHERN REACH FACILITY/MEDICAL CENTRE – DAY

Kane lies on a bed. Surrounded by the tubes, lines, and the machinery of life support.

His skin is ivory. Steam wreathes his mouth as he gently exhales.

Kane is being tended by a Nurse in a full biohazard suit.

Lena and Dr Ventress watch from behind an observation window. The edges of the glass are frosted with ice crystals.

INT. SOUTHERN REACH FACILITY/MEDICAL CENTRE –
DAY

On Dr Ventress and Lena's side of the observation window:

DR VENTRESS
I want you to know: missions into the Shimmer are
volunteer basis. It was his decision to go in.

LENA
Induced coma, life-support. None of that will save his life.

DR VENTRESS
I'm afraid not.

Beat.

Lena – we need to come to an agreement about what to
do with you. I'd rather not lock you up again.

LENA
But you're not going to let me go home.

DR VENTRESS
Do you want to go home?

*Lena looks to Kane, vignetted through the frosting on the edges
of the glass.*

LENA
I want to stay with him.

DR VENTRESS
Then I have a solution. You're a biologist. We sequestered
you from Johns Hopkins. This is your first day at Southern
Reach.

Dr Ventress watches Lena.

LENA
I join you here? At this place.

DR VENTRESS
I don't actually see an alternative. For either of us.

EXT. SOUTHERN REACH FACILITY — NIGHT

The facility is picked out in the moonlight.

A row of floodlights along the perimeter wall illuminate the wasteground and the tree line.

EXT. SOUTHERN REACH FACILITY/ROOF — NIGHT

Lena stands on the flat roof of the Southern Reach Facility, leaning against the guard rail.

She's holding the silver locket containing Kane's photo in her hand. Gazing at it.

There are a few others from the facility dotted around the area. Talking in small groups, or standing alone.

One of those small groups, seated around a table sharing a beer, is made up of three women.

They are:

Anya Thorensen: a handsome woman in her early thirties. Close-cropped hair, wearing a white vest that shows muscled arms. She has a very distinctive tattoo encircling her forearm, depicting an ouroboros – a snake eating its tail.

Cass Sheppard: late thirties, glasses, hair tied back. No pretension, no glamour, no ostentation.

Josie Radek: mid- to late-twenties, but feels younger. She has the sheltered quality of people who passed straight from school to college to doctorate. She wears long sleeves, pulled over her hands, with arms crossed. A picture of self-defence.

Thorensen is watching Lena.

After a couple of moments, she detaches herself from the other two, and approaches.

Lena, gazing at the locket, doesn't notice.

THORENSEN

Hey.

Lena looks up, and closes the locket with a soft snap before
Thorensen can see the image inside.

LENA

. . . Hey.

THORENSEN

Am I intruding?

Lena slips the necklace back over her head.

LENA

No, not at all.

Thorensen smiles.

THORENSEN

Cool. So, I was working one of the scanner stations when
you ran by, breaking land-speed records.

LENA

. . . Ah.

THORENSEN

Then I saw you here, alone. And I figured you were feeling
weird and awkward.

LENA

Somewhat, I guess.

THORENSEN

Right. But don't. This place is freaky. One in ten here get
the orange jumpsuit. The ice-cool professionals you see
here? On the inside they're curled up in foetal positions,
making cooing noises.

Lena smiles.

Thorensen holds out her hand.

I'm Anya.

Lena shakes.

LENA

Lena.

37

THORENSEN
Good to meet you. Come join us.

Thorensen gestures towards Radek and Sheppard.

Say hi to my crew.

EXT. SOUTHERN REACH FACILITY/ROOF – CONTINUOUS

Thorensen brings Lena to Sheppard and Radek.

THORENSEN
Guys, this is Lena. Lena, meet Josie Radek –

RADEK
Hi.

THORENSEN
– and Cass Sheppard.

SHEPPARD
Actually, we already met. But it was a little hurried.

*A moment of realisation for Lena – Sheppard is the female
scientist she sent crashing to the floor in her run through the
observation area.*

LENA
Oh, I knocked you over, didn't I? I am so sorry.

Sheppard laughs.

SHEPPARD
It's already forgotten. Come on, sit.

*Lena pulls up a chair, while Thorensen reaches beside the table
to an ice-box.*

THORENSEN
What do you want? I got beer. Say beer.

LENA
Beer's good.

Thorensen hands Lena a bottle.

SHEPPARD

So first day at the Southern Reach.

LENA

Have you all been here a long time?

SHEPPARD

Right from the start. I'm a geologist. I've been testing the magnetic fields around the boundary, which is like using confetti to test a hurricane. But I stayed on.

THORENSEN

Me: ten months. Paramedic, Chicago. Joined an NGO, and my application got flagged, and Southern Reach got in touch.

Lena looks to Radek.

RADEK

Only two months. I'm a physicist. I came here straight from my Cambridge post-doc.

SHEPPARD

She's very smart.

THORENSEN

But never been kissed.

RADEK
(to Lena)

I have been kissed.

THORENSEN

Never been *kissed*.

Sheppard changes the subject.

SHEPPARD

So what's your story, Lena?

LENA

I'm from Johns Hopkins. Biologist.

THORENSEN

A biologist? Damn.

RADEK

Ha!

SHEPPARD

Told you she was smart.

LENA

I don't follow.

SHEPPARD

We had a bet on your profession. Josie had biologist.

Thorensen takes a twenty out of her pocket and slides it to Radek.

THORENSEN

You're uncanny.

SHEPPARD

I had law enforcement. But maybe that's just because you knocked me on my back.

THORENSEN

And I had you as single.

Thorensen winks.

In case you want to put me on my back too.

SHEPPARD

Anya, stop hitting on everyone.

THORENSEN

Fuck that. Under the circumstances, I think I'm more than allowed a few last rolls of the dice.

Lena takes a sip of her beer.

LENA

Under what circumstances?

The other three women exchange a glance. And the sudden pause seems to provide the answer to the question.

Even before Sheppard answers, we know.

                    SHEPPARD
Yeah. Crazy as it sounds –

                    THORENSEN
Crazy as it is.

Sheppard nods towards the floodlit treeline.

                    SHEPPARD
– we're headed that way.

*Put so simply, it's as if the temperature of the conversation
suddenly drops.*

                    LENA
You're going into the Shimmer?

                    THORENSEN
Six days and counting.

Beat.

                    LENA
You three.

                    RADEK
Four. Ventress.

                    LENA
Dr Ventress?

                    SHEPPARD
Team leader.

                    LENA
All women.

                    RADEK
Scientists.

                    SHEPPARD
The previous teams have been largely military.

                    LENA
What do you think happened to them?

THORENSEN

There are two theories about what goes wrong inside the Shimmer. One, something in there kills them. Two, they go crazy and kill each other.

LENA

. . . What do you think?

THORENSEN

I think testosterone has been shit out of luck. So I'm good with the oestrogen.

RADEK

There was one military guy who made it out. The sergeant.

THORENSEN

You heard about the state he's in? Doesn't sound like luck to me.

On Lena. On the verge of stating her connection to Kane.

But she hesitates.

Then looks over to the distant floodlit treeline.

LENA

. . . No. It doesn't.

THORENSEN

Ouch. This is getting morbid.

Thorensen reaches back to the ice-box. Pulls out a fresh bottle and uses the lip of the table to pop the cap. Then slides it to Radek.

What say you all get drunk and we make out?

Sheppard's laughter floats across the viewing platform.

Stars vibrate through the Shimmer.

INT. MEDICAL CENTRE – NIGHT

Outside Kane's isolation tent, the biohazard-suited Nurse sits asleep.

Kane lies, deep in coma, breathing gently.

Reveal – through the plastic sheeting, Lena entering the medical centre quietly.

She approaches the plastic sheeting. Gazes at Kane through it.

It's not enough – being so near, not being able touch him.

Her eyes flick to the sleeping Nurse.

Cut to:

Lena opening the seal to the oxygen tent, and slipping inside.

INT. OXYGEN TENT – CONTINUOUS

Lena sits on the bed beside Kane.

Touches his cheek.

Speaks quietly.

> LENA
> I know what I have to do.

Beat.

> I'm going to go in there. I'm going to find out what
> happened to you. And I'm going to make it better.

She takes his hand.

> Kane. I'm sorry.

Beat.

> (*Whispers.*) I'm so sorry.

EXT. SOUTHERN REACH FACILITY – DAY

Daylight over the Southern Reach.

Looking back towards Dr Ventress's office, in which we can see Lena and Dr Ventress.

INT. SOUTHERN REACH FACILITY/VENTRESS OFFICE –
CONTINUOUS

Lena sits opposite the desk.

*Dr Ventress stands by the window, looking towards the
Shimmer.*

> DR VENTRESS
> So you didn't tell them about your connection to Sergeant
> Kane.

> LENA
> I assumed it would be in conflict with my cover story.

Lena pauses.

> LENA
> And I thought it would complicate everything.

> DR VENTRESS
> . . . What would it complicate?

Lena leaves this question. Instead, asks one of her own.

> LENA
> Why are you going into the Shimmer?

> DR VENTRESS
> The mission statement is to reach the believed source of the
> Shimmer: the lighthouse. Enter, acquire data, and return.

> LENA
> But I don't think that's your mission statement.

> DR VENTRESS
> . . . No.

Dr Ventress looks at the distant treeline.

> I've been watching the phenomenon for a while now.
> Others enter. I watch it grow closer. There's only so long
> one can do that.

Beat.

> It's not that it doesn't frighten me.

                              LENA

But you just need to know what's inside.

                          DR VENTRESS

Yes. I do.

                              LENA

So do I.

Dr Ventress turns to Lena. Sees her level gaze.

                          DR VENTRESS

Ah. So that's the complication.

The doctor smiles faintly.

You want to come with us. Soldier-scientist. You can fight.
You can learn. You can save him.

                              LENA

I can try.

INT. INTERROGATION ROOM – DAY

Lomax, gazing at Lena.

                             LOMAX

Requesting to join a mission into the Shimmer. All other
missions have failed. And the only survivor is barely
surviving. (*Flat.*) A brave choice.

                              LENA

It wasn't a choice.

                             LOMAX

Go on.

                              LENA

I'd failed him. I owed him.

                             LOMAX

How?

LENA

How? In the way people always fail their partners. Because
I'd been afraid he wouldn't come back. Because I spent so
much time alone.

LOMAX

I'm just trying to understand what drove you.

LENA

I don't know what drove me. I never do. These are just
things to say. I'd failed him. So I owed him. So I went in.

Cut to:

*The team crossing the deforested area, approaching the
Shimmer.*

EXT. SKY — DAWN

Colour seeps out of cloud forms.

EXT. DEFORESTED AREA — DAWN

Tree forms melt through the Shimmer.

EXT. DEFORESTED AREA — DAWN

The team walk in single file away from the Southern Reach.

All carry backpacks and automatic rifles.

*Ahead of them is the dusty scrubland of the deforested area.
Beyond is the undulating treeline.*

Dr Ventress leads.

Then Thorensen, then Sheppard, then Radek, then Lena.

When Dr Ventress reaches the treeline, she stops.

Then turns, to look back at Lena.

They lock eyes through the melting air.

Cut to black.

Caption:

PART TWO – AREA X

Cut to:

EXT. HOUSE/BEDROOM – DAY

The full moon, hanging in a clear blue daylight sky.

The same image that distracted Lena as she taught her medical students, now framed by the window of Lena's bedroom.

Lena and Kane lie in bed.

Kane watches the pale orb.

Lena watches him.

>   LENA
> You aren't talking to me.

>   KANE
> . . . Sorry. Zoned out.

>   LENA
> Thinking about the next mission?

>   KANE
> No. Just watching the moon. It always feels weird, catching sight of it in daylight.

Lena smiles.

>   LENA
> Like God made a mistake. Left the hall lights on.

>   KANE
> God doesn't make mistakes. It's somewhat key to the whole being-a-God thing.

>   LENA
> Pretty sure he does.

KANE

You know he's listening, right?

Beat.

LENA

Take a cell, circumvent the Hayflick limit, and you can prevent senescence.

KANE

I was about to make the exact same point.

LENA

It means the cell doesn't grow old. It becomes immortal. Keeps dividing. Doesn't die. So where we see the aging process as natural, it's actually a fault in our genes . . .

KANE

It turns me on when you patronise me.

LENA

And without it, I would stay looking like this –

She indicates herself.

– forever.

KANE

It's possible that constitutes a mistake.

He kisses her.

She breaks off.

. . . Are you going to tell me where you're heading this time?

He doesn't.

I know there's something strange about the mission.

KANE

. . . Why?

LENA

Because the silence around it is louder than usual.

Beat.

Kind of angling for a clue here.

KANE

Uh-huh.

LENA

So?

Kane sighs.

KANE

We'll be under the same hemisphere.

LENA

What does that tell me?

KANE

It tells you: if you step outside and look up, you'll know we're seeing the same stars.

Lena looks at Kane.

LENA

Holy fucking shit.

KANE

. . . What?

LENA

Are you kidding? Is that what you think I do when you're away?

KANE

I'm just saying –

LENA

You think I come out into the garden, pining, looking up at the sky?

Lena puts her hand on her chest. Mimics herself.

To think my darling Kane is looking at this self-same Moon. O my distant celestial friend –

Kane laughs. Shoves her sideways.

Lena keeps going.

> LENA

– please care for my beloved . . .

Kane grabs her. Tries to stop her talking.

> LENA

– my brave soldier . . .

> KANE

Jesus – you know what you are? You're disrespectful, not just to your former comrades of the armed forces –

Lena yelps as he starts tickling her.

– but also the President.

> LENA
> (*between gasps*)

You forgot the flag!

> KANE

Oh, I'm getting to the motherfucking flag.

Lena can no longer talk because he's tickling her too hard.

She becomes helpless with laughter.

> LENA

My hero.

> KANE

Screw you.

> LENA

Okay.

They start kissing.

With passion.

Cut to:

The full moon.

Suspended in the blue. Crater patterns only faintly visible in daylight.

Then –

– the moon shimmers.

And then, like a cell under a microscope –

– the moon starts to divide.

Cut to:

INT. TENT – DAY

Lena, waking with a jolt.

Looking around. Surrounded by bright orange.

Taking a moment to understand she is inside a tent.

EXT. FOREST CLEARING/CAMPSITE – CONTINUOUS

Lena unzips the front flap of her tent and climbs out –

– to discover a campsite. Five small tents, circled around a burned-out fire.

The campsite is positioned in a grassy clearing, deep inside a forest.

Just in front of Lena, Thorensen and Sheppard sit surrounded by packets of food.

A little distance away, Radek is looking at a piece of electronic equipment.

And Dr Ventress is gazing up at the sky.

The sun and clouds are seen through the familiar mirage-like distortion – as if the Shimmer is like a dome structure, which we are now inside.

Lena looks stunned.

> LENA
>
> . . . What the hell?

Thorensen and Sheppard look round.

THORENSEN

You're finally awake.

LENA

Sorry, you're going to have to give me a moment. I'm a little . . . disoriented.

SHEPPARD

Join the club.

THORENSEN

You don't remember setting up camp, right?

LENA

. . . I don't remember anything, after we reached the treeline.

SHEPPARD

None of us do. But check your boots and pants. They'll be wet and covered in mud. And we've been doing an inventory of the food. From the depletion, we've been out here for at least forty-eight hours.

LENA

That's not possible.

Radek walks over, looking nervous.

RADEK

Guys.

Radek pulls her short-wave radio from her belt. Gives it a burst.

It plays static.

I've been checking all my comms and navigation equipment. None of it is working properly. Like, I can switch on the sat and the GPS, and they boot up fine. No problem with the electronics. But there's no signal. Even though we've probably got twenty satellites above us right now – nothing. And check this out.

Radek holds up a magnetic compass. The needle is spinning slowly.

There is excitement in Radek's voice. And a note of panic.

So we've got no compass, no comms, no coordinates, and no landmarks.

> SHEPPARD
>
> Josie, be cool. We know we're in the state park. We go south, we hit the ocean. Then we can follow the shoreline until we hit the perimeter wall.

> RADEK
>
> But how do we know what's south?

Sheppard stands. Pulls up her sleeve. Shows her wristwatch.

> SHEPPARD
>
> Hour hand at the sun. Split the difference between the hour hand and twelve.

As she's talking, she's doing.

She points into the forest.

South.

Radek and Lena exchange a glance.

Dr Ventress shows no sense of anxiety about the situation. She seems almost serene.

> DR VENTRESS
>
> Good. So we're oriented. And we weren't really expecting the comms equipment to work, were we? After three years of expeditions, and three years of radio silence.

She gestures at the tents.

We're all awake. Let's pack up and get moving. It's already late. We don't want to lose any more of the day.

EXT. SWAMP – DAY

The five women are walking in ankle-deep water.

It's hot. Heavy backpacks. Heavy weapons. Hard going.

It's also impossible to gauge the depth of the swamp.

Thorensen suddenly steps into a hole. Sinks into the black water, up to her knees.

> THORENSEN
> Fucking damn it.

Lena offers Thorensen a hand. Hauls her out.

> Now I know why we've all got amnesia. Why would you want to remember this shit-hole?

Thorensen marches ahead, soaked, pissed off.

Lena looks around.

Sees the cypress trees with their fanned-out roots, Spanish moss on the branches, dappled sunlight through the high canopy. All reflected in the glassy water.

Radek has a hand-held camera out, and is filming Lena looking at the view.

Cut to Radek's camera point-of-view –

– as Lena turns to Radek. To the lens.

> LENA
> It's beautiful.

Cut to:

Radek. She finishes the shot, and stows the camera.

> RADEK
> Me too. I've never seen anything like this before. I'm not really the outdoors type.

They start walking again.

                              LENA
So what type are you?

                              RADEK
Oh, you know. The indoors buried-in-a-book type. Just
like you had me figured.

                              LENA
I'm kind of that type too.

Radek glances sideways.

                              RADEK
No. You aren't.

Lena smiles.

                              LENA
What's in the books?

                              RADEK
My thing is the life cycle of stars. Nebulas to supernovas.

                              LENA
Typical physicist. I can't deal with those parameters. I like
the life-cycle of cells. Nice and short.

                              RADEK
Still a cycle.

Up ahead –

– Sheppard has seen something.

A structure, through the trees.

And a strange intense scattering of colour.

Sheppard calls back to the others.

                              SHEPPARD
Over here!

EXT. SWAMP/FISHING HUT – DAY

The five women approach the bank of the swamp.

Ahead is a long trailer-like hut.

It sits on the water, supported by oil-barrel floats.

Some of the barrels have been punctured or collapsed, meaning the back half of the structure has sunk into the water like a sinking boat.

A jetty connects the door with the land.

And from the land, there is a dense carpet of white flowers. They cover the short jetty and push up the side of the building like a snow drift.

Further along the bank, there are two fibreglass boats, pulled up on the shore.

Sheppard and Thorensen go to investigate them –

– as Lena slips off her pack, puts down her gun, and crouches by the flowers to take a closer look.

Although the flowers are all white, the actual blooms are intensely varied. Some large with broad petals. Some small and glass-like. Some like orchids, some like jasmine.

LENA

. . . These are very strange.

DR VENTRESS

Why?

LENA

They're so different. To look at them, you wouldn't say they're the same species.

Lena pulls back an area of flowers to show the plant system beneath.

LENA

But they're all growing from the same branch structure. Not just the same species. The same plant.

RADEK

They're like snowflakes. Not one is the same.

56

                              LENA
It's like it's stuck in a continuous mutation.

                          DR VENTRESS
        A pathology?

*Lena picks a white flower with a delicate red stamen, and holds
it up.*

                              LENA
You'd sure as hell call it a pathology if you saw it in a
human.

While Lena studies the unusual petals –

– Radek has walked up the jetty to the front door of the hut.

She peers inside the door-frame.

*The interior is dark. The windows and skylight are clouded with
dirt. Not much sunlight gets inside.*

*It looks like it was once a living dwelling, before it collapsed.
Now the floor slopes steeply into ink-black water. There appears
to be a rotten sofa floating near the back of the room.*

Thorensen calls from the bank.

                          THORENSEN
Anything interesting in there?

Radek turns back from the doorway.

                              RADEK
No. It's long abandoned. Maybe even before –

She cuts herself off in mid-sentence.

*Then she frowns slightly, and starts to turn, as if she has heard
something behind her.*

*Then suddenly Radek is yanked backwards by something. Hard.
And she vanishes into the black doorway of the hut, out of
sight.*

A confused beat on the women on the bank.

Lena rises.

LENA

Radek?

Silence.

Lena sets off up the jetty

LENA

Radek!

INT. FISHING HUT – CONTINUOUS

She reaches the door. Sees the half-submerged interior.

The darkness in the room is almost impenetrable.

And Radek simply isn't there.

Instead, there is a disturbance on the surface of the water. Something moving underneath.

LENA

What the fuck?

A moment later –

– Radek erupts out of the water.

She emerges by the sunken sofa, trying to hold on to the arm. Panic-stricken. Choking. Something appears to be trapping her, or holding her under.

RADEK

It's got my bag – it's got my bag – help me –

As Lena starts to move –

Radek's screams are abruptly knocked out of her –

– as something in the water viciously grabs her, snapping the young woman sideways like a rag doll.

Then sucking her back under the surface.

Radek is gone again.

58

Thorensen appears in the doorway.

THORENSEN

What's going on?

LENA

I don't know! Something's got her! Something in the water!

Lena goes deeper into the hut, wading into the ink liquid –

THORENSEN

Be careful!

LENA

Shine your light! I can't see shit!

Thorensen reaches for her belt. Gets her flashlight. Sweeps the beam into the hut –

– and finds the disturbance on the surface.

LENA

There!

Lena wades deeper in, and reaches underwater with her hand –

– and gets hold of something.

LENA

I've got her!

With a massive effort, Lena pulls, and as her hand breaks the surface, we can see it is locked with Radek's.

Now Radek's face just manages to clear the water – her nose and lips in the air, choking and gasping for air.

Then Sheppard is there beside Lena, and has got a hand to Radek too, and both women manage to pull Radek forwards.

Free from whatever was holding her.

Together, Sheppard and Lena haul Radek out of the hut, and into the daylight.

EXT. SWAMP/FISHING HUT – CONTINUOUS

The women get down the jetty to the bank.

We can see that Radek's waterlogged backpack has been partially shredded at the back.

> SHEPPARD
> What the hell is in there?

> LENA
> I don't know – something strong –

> THORENSEN
> Her bag's all ripped up –

Thorensen is interrupted by a massive pounding noise.

Something has just impacted hard against the interior of the hut – so hard the walls shake.

All five women turn –

– and a beat later there is a second huge impact. Ripples spread out from the sunken hut across the swamp water.

> THORENSEN
> . . . Shit.

The third impact never comes.

Instead, there is a scraping sound from inside the building.

And a moment later, something emerges from the doorway.

The head of a massive albino alligator.

Its hide is a dirty yellowed-ivory colour. It has raw and open lesions scarring the snout. Its eyes are pale, rimmed bright red, and clouded with a cataract-like surface.

The sight is nightmarish.

And a moment later, it is gone –

– because the huge beast has slipped out of the door, over the narrow jetty –

– and into the swamp.

A single silent beat.

. . . I think it's coming.

Ventress, Sheppard, and Thorensen raise their guns.

Lena's gun is over by her pack, by the flowers.

Radek is half collapsed, still gasping for breath.

A moment later, the alligator thrusts out of the water, lunging up the shore. Incredible speed. Massive jaws pulling open.

The women with weapons open fire –

– but the creature isn't apparently affected. It swipes sideways, striking Thorensen, knocking her backwards.

Then moves for Radek again, who is trapped by the weight of her sodden backpack.

Lena has managed to get to her gun.

She crouches, aims, and empties a clip into its side.

Rounds slam into the creature, but don't seem to even slow it. Instead, the impacts simply redirect the attention of the alligator from Radek to her.

It starts to move to Lena fast.

Lena desperately tries to jam in a new clip –

– as the alligator propels itself in her direction.

Just as the creature is about to reach her, head twisting, jaws opening, about to strike –

– the clip is driven home, and Lena cocks her gun and opens fire again –

– emptying this magazine at point blank range, directly down the alligator's throat.

The muzzle flash illuminates the interior. Bullets slam into the flesh.

Lena is joined by Sheppard, Thorensen and Dr Ventress.

In seconds, four women empty four magazines. Riddling the creature's head and torso.

After the last shot is fired, the alligator remains supported on its legs, jaws open, frozen for a moment, half out of the water.

Then the legs buckle.

And the jaws shut.

It's dead.

Cut to black.

INT. GATOR – DAY

In darkness, we hear Radek's voice.

Muffled.

> SHEPPARD
> (*out of shot*)
> Be careful! There might be a reflex!

> THORENSEN
> (*out of shot*)
> I think its reflex days are gone.

Sudden daylight –

– as we see the jaws being prized back open, from the point-of-view of the gullet.

We are inside the wet cave of the alligator's mouth, looking out over a slab of tongue, and jagged stalagmite/stalactite teeth.

Lena is peering in.

Behind her, we can see Radek and Dr Ventress.

Radek is filming on her small hand-held camera.

The jaw is being held open by Thorensen – who is wearing rubber surgical gloves.

> LENA

        . . . Whoa.

Lena sticks her head even further inside.

        It's exactly the same as the flowers.

We see what Lena sees through Radek's camera point-of-view.

Behind the row of teeth, there is a second row. Internal, folded backward slightly.

And behind the second row, there is a third, these almost flat.

> LENA

        Look at the teeth. Concentric rows. Something here is making big waves in the gene pool.

> SHEPPARD

        Sharks have teeth like that.

> DR VENTRESS

        A cross-breed?

> LENA

        You can't cross-breed between different species.

> THORENSEN
> (*strained*)

        Hey – that's all cool. But can you get your head the fuck out so we can let this go? It's kind of heavy.

A final beat on Lena's puzzled expression.

Then Lena nods.

> LENA

        Sure.

Lena retracts her head.

The jaw shuts with a wet thump.

Cut to:

INT. INTERROGATION ROOM – DAY

Lena and Lomax.

> LENA
>
> They were subtle at first. More extreme as we grew closer.

> LOMAX
>
> The mutations.

> LENA
>
> The corruptions of form. And duplicates of form.

> LOMAX
>
> Duplicates?

Lena looks down at the tattoo on her arm.

> LENA
>
> Doubles. Or echoes.

> LOMAX
>
> . . . It is possible these were hallucinations?

> LENA
>
> No. I wondered at first, but they were shared between all of us. (*Beat.*) It was dreamlike.

> LOMAX
>
> Frightening. Nightmarish.

Lena shakes her head.

> LENA
>
> Not always.

Cut to the boats, gliding through the swamps.

> (*Out of shot.*) Sometimes it was beautiful.

INT. SWAMP/FISHING HUT – DAY

Two boats paddle away from the fishing hut.

EXT. SWAMP – DAY

A tree in the swamp.

The trunk is clustered with fat mounds of moss, flourishing like petri-dish cultures.

They have bright colours. Not just greens, but intense reds, and purples, and rust colours.

They look like disease.

Cut to:

EXT. SWAMP – DAY

The flat-bottomed boats gliding over black water. Swampland floating by. Serene.

The first boat holds Dr Ventress, Radek and Thorensen, with Thorensen paddling.

Radek's ripped bag has been roughly taped to hold it together.

The second boat holds Sheppard and Lena.

While Sheppard paddles, Lena is preoccupied by a mark on her forearm.

It looks like a faint bruise.

Lena pushes at it with her thumb. Vaguely puzzled about where she picked it up.

> SHEPPARD

You hurt?

> LENA

Just a bruise. Guess I picked it up with that gator.

> SHEPPARD

Likely.

Beat.

So where did you learn to shoot?

LENA

I was in the military before I was an academic.

SHEPPARD

Air force?

LENA

Army. Seven years. Feels like a lifetime ago now.

SHEPPARD

All other lives were a lifetime ago. We were children. I was married. Which do you carry around your neck? A husband or a child?

Lena prepares to gets her internal story straight.

Then looks round.

LENA

A husband. He was in the army too. It's where we met.

SHEPPARD

Was in the army. But he didn't quit.

LENA

. . . No.

Lena doesn't want to lie to Sheppard – but does.

LENA

KIA.

It's almost the truth.

SHEPPARD

Well, there had to be something.

LENA

. . . What do you mean?

SHEPPARD

Volunteering for this – it's not something you do if your life is in perfect harmony.

Sheppard nods towards the other boat.

We're all damaged goods here. Anya is a teetotal, therefore an addict. Josie wears long sleeves because she doesn't want you to see the pale scars on her forearms.

LENA

She's tried to kill herself?

SHEPPARD

I think the opposite. Trying to feel alive.

LENA

What about Ventress?

SHEPPARD

No friends, no family, no partner, no children. No concession in her at all. It's like she's defined by what isn't there.

LENA

She's alone.

SHEPPARD

More than most.

Beat.

Sheppard catches Lena's eye.

You can ask.

LENA

You.

SHEPPARD

I also lost someone. But not a husband – a daughter. Leukaemia.

LENA

. . . I'm sorry.

SHEPPARD

Yes.

Beat.

In a way, it's two bereavements. There's my beautiful girl, and the person I once was.

Beat.

I know you understand.

Lena can't answer.

They lapse back into silence.

Behind them, Sheppard's oar strokes leave a gentle disturbance on the water.

Cut to:

EXT. SWAMP — DAY

The two boats gliding towards a shoreline.

Thorensen in the lead boat, eyes narrowing.

> THORENSEN
> We got something here . . .

Above the trees, a guard tower can be seen.

EXT. ABANDONED BASE — DAY

The five women walk through a checkpoint, into a collection of abandoned military buildings. Single-storey barrack huts and storage depots, all are surrounded by a double chain-link fence, barbed wire, and guard towers.

Nature has been busy reclaiming the area. Tall grasses push through cracks in the tarmac. The concrete is stained with rain and dark algae.

And as with the trees in the swamp, brightly coloured lichens and mosses bloom on the buildings.

> LENA
> More mutations.

> RADEK
> They're everywhere.

With field kit, Lena takes a sample with a scalpel, and seals it in a plastic vial.

LENA

They look malignant. Like tumours.

Sheppard is checking her map.

SHEPPARD

At least now we know where we are. This was the previous Southern Reach headquarters, before the Shimmer swallowed it.

Radek exhales.

RADEK

Great. Then we're not lost any more.

THORENSEN

Feels like a good place to stay the night.

Dr Ventress points to a low building up ahead.

DR VENTRESS

That used to be the mess hall. We'll billet there.

INT. ABANDONED BASE/MESS HALL — DAY

The door to the mess hall opens, and the five women enter.

Light pushes through the grimy windows, and the foliage that has grown up outside.

It illuminates a large space, with a dark kitchen area at the back. A few scattered tables and bench remain.

Thorensen pulls off her bag.

THORENSEN

I've slept in worse.

SHEPPARD

. . . Really?

THORENSEN

Well, maybe not worse . . .

Lena has walked further into the room.

And found something.

LENA

Guys. Check this out.

The others come to join her.

Reveal that an area of the mess hall has been repurposed.

Radio equipment and a couple of military backpacks are stacked against the wall.

Beside them is an armoury of sorts. A couple of automatic rifles, an ammo box, and a belt-fed machine gun.

THORENSEN

People are here?

LENA

Or were.

Sheppard takes a closer look at the weapon stack. All are covered in fine dust.

SHEPPARD

Yeah, I'm going with the past tense.

And a little further down, the wall has been neatly graffitied.

It shows a list of names, and beside the names are twenty-four-hour clock times.

Three of the names are crossed out.

There is also a rough map – boxes for buildings, and a dotted line for the perimeter fence.

Lena reads from the list.

LENA

Peyton, Mayer, Shelley . . .

One of the names on the wall is Kane's. Lena doesn't read it out.

DR VENTRESS

They were soldiers on the previous expedition. Looks like they were using this room as a base of operations.

                              RADEK
Why are some of the names crossed out?

                            SHEPPARD
Let's not jump to conclusions.

Lena frowns.

                              LENA
I'm not sure. Maybe we should.

She taps the map.

                              LENA
This is a plan-view of the base. This is the building we're
in. And I think the times by the names are a guard rota.

Lena glances back at the others.

                              LENA
If they were guarding the perimeter, we should too.

                           THORENSEN
Copy that.

                           DR VENTRESS
Perhaps this will tell us something.

The others look round.

Dr Ventress is standing by a table, positioned against the wall.

*On the table there is a clear plastic envelope, of the sort for
keeping maps dry. It has been weighted to the table with a
handgun.*

Someone has written on the plastic.

Dr Ventress reads the words out loud.

                           DR VENTRESS
'For those that follow' . . .

Beat.

I believe that means us.

Dr Ventress picks up the envelope, and tips it on to the table.

A single object slides out.

An SD memory card.

Cut to:

INT. ABANDONED BASE/MESS HALL – CONTINUOUS

The five women, standing around Radek's camera, as she inserts the SD card, clips shut the card hatch, and powers the camera up.

RADEK

. . . It's working.

Cut to:

INT. SCREEN

Close-up on the screen of Radek's camera.

The video starts.

At first, abstract. Static-like distortions against darkness. Particles. Swirling. Seeming to find human forms at brief moments, like ghosts flickering across the screen.

Then the images suddenly resolve.

It's night.

We are in what seems to be a room.

The walls are tiled.

And by the wall there are four soldiers.

One of them, Mayer, is sitting on a chair.

Shirtless. Slumped forwards. Blood is smeared down his chest. Some wet, some dry.

He's making a soft moaning sound.

He is flanked by Shelley and Peyton. Their uniforms are filthy.

Both have beards. The room is lit by their flashlights.

The fourth soldier has his back to us.

He's a silhouette, but we can see he's holding a combat knife.

Then the fourth soldier glances back over his shoulder.

At the camera.

At us.

And we find we are looking at Kane.

Cut to:

INT. ABANDONED BASE/MESS HALL – CONTINUOUS

Lena.

Freezing at the sight of her husband.

She shoots a glance at Dr Ventress.

Dr Ventress doesn't look back.

Cut back to:

INT. SCREEN

Kane.

He stares down the barrel of the lens.

He looks wired.

KANE

Ready?

CAMERAMAN

Yes.

Kane turns back to Mayer.

Then leans in to Mayer. And starts to cut open his stomach.

Cut to:

INT. ABANDONED BASE/MESS HALL – CONTINUOUS

The faces of the women watching.

Radek, wide-eyed, hand clamped to her mouth.

> RADEK
> Oh shit, shit – what's he doing?

INT. SCREEN

Kane makes a vertical cut.

Then two horizontal.

It's not an attack: it's more like field surgery.

Mayer's moaning sound raises in pitch.

It remains unintelligible.

Then Kane pulls back.

Mayer's trousers and Kane's hands are soaked in blood.

Kane wipes sweat off his forehead with the back of his arm.

> KANE
> There.

He looks back at the camera.

He points with the tip of his knife.

The camera moves to Mayer.

A large flap has been cut in his stomach, and pulled down.

Peyton shines his flashlight in the cavity.

We see Mayer's intestines.

And they are moving.

At first, it looks as if there is something alive inside the coils.

Then we realise it is the coils themselves that are moving.

The ribbed shape looks suddenly the segments of a huge, white, living worm.

In the background, the raised pitch of Mayer's moaning has eventually become a scream.

The film abruptly ends.

Cut to:

INT. ABANDONED BASE/MESS HALL – CONTINUOUS

Radek retching outside the doorway of the mess hall, framed by the bright sunlight.

Dr Ventress is locked in private thought.

Lena is ashen. Shaking.

Thorensen also looks like she is struggling to hold it together.

> THORENSEN
> Okay. So at least now we know what happened to the previous team. They went insane.

> SHEPPARD
> But there was something alive inside that man.

> THORENSEN
> No. That was a trick of the light.

> SHEPPARD
> What?

> THORENSEN
> Ten years, I was a paramedic. You scrape people off roads, you see weird shit. You think it doesn't make sense.

Radek wipes her mouth.

> RADEK
> His insides were moving.

> THORENSEN
> It's shock. A shock response.

> SHEPPARD
> Watch it again.

THORENSEN

I'm not fucking watching that again!

SHEPPARD

There was a worm. A tapeworm, or –

Sheppard breaks off.

Dr Ventress has started walking. She heads into a dark corridor off the mess hall, lit at the far end by daylight.

SHEPPARD

Where are you going?

INT. ABANDONED BASE/TILED CORRIDOR – CONTINUOUS

Dr Ventress walks down a white-tiled corridor.

Behind her, at the far end, the other four women appear.

INT. ABANDONED BASE/EMPTY SWIMMING POOL – CONTINUOUS

Dr Ventress enters a large space.

She is followed by the other women.

It's the same room as in the film clip, but now seen in daylight.

And now we can see that what seemed to be tiled walls was in fact the inside of a massive indoor swimming pool, drained of water.

At the deep end is what is what is left of Mayer's body.

It is as if he has been very slowly exploding in the weeks or months since he was cut open.

The brightly coloured lichen-tumours on the sides of trees and the buildings have blossomed inside him.

The lower part of his desiccated body is still seated on the chair.

But his upper body has been pulled apart. His arms have been dislocated from the shoulders, and pushed up the wall by the growth.

His skull is four or five foot above where his neck would have been.

The women climb down into the pool and approach the corpse.

Lena uses the muzzle of her gun to touch at the growth.

It gives only slightly.

THORENSEN
What is it? Plant, or . . . what?

LENA
Maybe a mould of some kind. I don't know.

Silence.

RADEK
. . . I don't want to stay here tonight.

No one says anything.

I don't want to stay here tonight!

DR VENTRESS
I don't think we have a choice. It's too late in the day for us to move on.

RADEK
Please –

SHEPPARD
Hey.

Sheppard puts a hand on Radek's face. Gently redirecting the younger woman's gaze away from the corpse.

We won't stay in the mess hall. We'll find another building. And figure out our guard rota.

Lena stares at the lichen-tumours pushing between Mayer's splayed ribcage.

77

Along the edges of the tumour there are tiny fronds.

As Lena gazes, there is the slightest sense that they are moving.

Close on the fractal shape.

Then cut to:

EXT. ABANDONED BASE – DUSK

The five women walking across the base, towards the guard tower.

Cut to:

EXT. HOUSE/BEDROOM – DAWN

Lena's face.

Asleep. In darkness.

Then light flooding on to her closed eyes.

Stirring her.

In the foreground –

– a glass of orange juice is laid down. On to a bedside table.

Lena blinks herself awake . . .

. . . to see her bedroom.

And Kane drawing the curtains.

Then turning to her.

Lena smiles drowsily.

                    LENA
    That's a nice surprise.

She runs a hand along the empty space in the bed

    Hey. Why aren't you here?

Kane hesitates slightly.

Then sits, not lies, on the bed next to her.

She knows: something isn't right.

> LENA

What?

> KANE

I'm leaving a day early.

> LENA

Today?

> KANE

Now.

Beat.

> LENA

. . . Shit.

Lena props herself up.

I had our whole day planned. We were going to drive
out to –

> KANE
> (*cuts in*)

I can't. We can't.

Lena reaches out with her hand. Takes his.

> LENA

Well, can we at least –

He pulls his hand back.

> LENA

. . . 'Now' means 'right now'.

> KANE

Yeah.

A beat.

> LENA

. . . What is it?

Kane doesn't answer for a moment.

Then he looks at her.

> KANE

I do love you, Lena.

Lena frowns.

It's not that he's lying. It's that it's presented as a statement of fact.

> LENA

. . . I love you too.

On Kane.

Gazing back at her flatly.

Giving nothing back. Unreachable.

Cut to:

INT. ABANDONED BASE/GUARD TOWER – NIGHT

Lena's eyes, flicking open.

Echoing the image of her waking that we just saw. But this time, she's in the top of the guard tower: a small square room, with windows on all four sides, surrounded by a platform and rail. Through the windows there are stars, deforming subtly through the Shimmer.

On the floor, she sees Thorensen, Radek, and Sheppard, asleep on their unrolled bedding.

Cut to:

Close-up images of the sample Lena took from the 'tumours'.

Strange cellular shapes, strange colours. None of them quite still. Moving almost imperceptibly slowly.

Cut to:

Lena, sitting over her field microscope. Lit from the light below the slide.

She sits up. Stretches. Rubs her eyes.

Then notices Sheppard is awake, and watching her.

Sheppard whispers:

> SHEPPARD
> Is the mystery unravelling?

Lena exhales. Whispers.

> LENA
> Something's unravelling.

Sheppard smiles.

> SHEPPARD
> I think you're doing okay.

Lena glances at Radek.

> LENA
> Good she's getting some rest.

> SHEPPARD
> Yeah – with the help of a little sedative.

> LENA
> How about you? Get any sleep?

> SHEPPARD
> Some. But think I'd need a horse-tranq to properly knock
> me out. I'm at least as freaked as Josie. Just hiding it better.

Beat.

> LENA
> I'll go check on Ventress.

> SHEPPARD
> You got it.

EXT. ABANDONED BASE/GUARD TOWER – CONTINUOUS

*When Lena exits the small room, we realise we are in the guard
tower that the women saw over the treetops, as they first
approached the base.*

The tower is on the edge of the abandoned facility. The starlight doesn't illuminate much, but we can just about make out the chain-link perimeter fence, and beyond it, the black shape of the forest.

Lena makes her way down the spiral stairs to the base of the tower –

– where Dr Ventress is sitting, studying a map by torchlight.

> DR VENTRESS
> What are you doing up? You're not due to relieve me until three a.m.

> LENA
> I'm done sleeping for the night.

> DR VENTRESS
> In that case, you might as well take a look at this.

Dr Ventress taps way-point positions on the map.

> We're here. This is where I think we camped last night. And here's the lighthouse. Judging by the distance we covered today, we won't reach it tomorrow. But south-west from here –

She indicates a new position.

> – is Ville Perdu. A small community, evacuated two years ago. I think we should aim there for tomorrow night. Then pick up the road to the coast.

Lena says nothing.

Dr Ventress notices the non-response.

She looks up at Lena from the map and the torchlight.

> I wanted to say: when you didn't tell the team about your connection to Sergeant Kane, I wasn't sure it was the right thing to do. But now I believe it was. I'm not sure how they would have reacted, after seeing that film.

Beat.

LENA

Why did my husband volunteer for a suicide mission?

DR VENTRESS

. . . Is that what you think we're doing? Committing suicide?

LENA

You must have profiled him. And assessed him. And he must have told you.

DR VENTRESS

So you're asking me as a psychologist.

LENA

Yes.

DR VENTRESS

Then, as a psychologist, I'd say you're confusing suicide with self-destruction. Almost none of us commit suicide, and almost all of us self-destruct. Somehow, in some part of our lives. We drink, or smoke. We destabilise the happy job –

Beat.

– or happy marriage.

Lena reacts. Uncertain whether this was targeted at her.

Dr Ventress continues.

But these aren't decisions. They're impulses. And in fact, as a biologist, you may be better placed to explain them than me.

LENA

What do you mean?

DR VENTRESS

Isn't self-destruction coded into us? Programmed into each cell.

The words hang.

And Lena is spared having to find a reply –

– by a strange noise, from somewhere in the darkness.

A soft moaning.

It's a little distant. Feels like it comes from the forest outside the perimeter fence.

Almost could be wind. Or could be animal. But it's oddly reminiscent of the sound Mayer made before Kane cut him open.

> LENA
>
> . . . What was that?

> DR VENTRESS
>
> I don't know.

The noise subsides.

The two women stay motionless for a few beats, listening.

Then relax slightly.

> Maybe a –

Dr Ventress is cut off by another noise.

A popping.

A tearing.

Not organic. Metallic. And surprisingly loud.

Lena unslings her rifles and raises it, switching on the night-vision scope.

Cut to:

The green-white view.

Scanning the tree line, through the fence.

> DR VENTRESS
>
> You see anything?

> LENA
>
> No, just –

Lena breaks off.

Yes.

Through the scope, there is something.

A large hole in the perimeter fence.

The chain-link twisted, pulled open.

Cut to:

Sheppard coming down the stairs of the guard tower, holding her weapon and a flashlight.

SHEPPARD
What's going on? I heard a noise.

LENA
Something's just come through the fence.

DR VENTRESS
What do you mean, through the fence?

Lena dips the gun.

LENA
Through. It's ripped open like a fucking zipper.

SHEPPARD
But what could do that?

LENA
Something big.

Another noise.

And this is organic. It's a thump of movement.

Then a panting breath. A snort.

And it feels very close.

The three women freeze.

A beat.

Then Sheppard lifts her flashlight.

Points it straight in front of her.

And illuminates a huge creature –

– less than two metres away.

It looks something like a black bear. But it's twice the size it should be.

On its body, patches of fur hang like the Spanish moss on the swamp-oak branches.

Much of the body is hairless, with pigmentation abnormalities, giving it an oddly mutated but human quality.

And it's up on its hind legs. Standing like a man, towering over Sheppard and Lena. Blotting out the stars.

Then it opens its jaws, revealing a pink, deformed maw.

It is a terrifying and transfixing sight.

SHEPPARD

. . . Shit.

The next moment – with shocking speed – the bear lunges downwards –

– at Sheppard.

There is a glimpse of her being pulled to the side, and almost compressed. Like a glimpse of someone being hit by a car.

Then the flashlight winks out.

And Sheppard is gone.

Sucked into a rush of movement and blackness.

Lena, who has hardly had time to draw breath, now reacts.

LENA

Sheppard!

No answer.

Lena clamps the night-scope to her eye, scanning desperately.

Sees something massive in the darkness, moving fast, back towards the fence. A glimpse of Sheppard, dragged like a rag doll.

Then it's gone. The creature, and Sheppard, have vanished.

LENA

SHEPPARD!

Thorensen and Radek appear at the base of the guard tower, holding their guns.

THORENSEN

What's going on?

LENA

Sheppard's gone! She was right here next to me – and something took her! It was like a bear, or –

Sudden screaming.

High, desperate. And sustained.

It's Sheppard. But she's nowhere close. It's from the trees.

THORENSEN

. . . Holy fuck.

Lena and Dr Ventress start running toward the sound.

They reach the break in the fence.

But the forest beyond is immeasurably massive and dark, and the screams are from deep inside.

Lena calls out –

LENA

SHEPPARD!

Sheppard's shrieking continues.

Then –

– abruptly stops.

EXT. THE SHIMMER – DAY

Daybreak, through the shimmer.

INT. ABANDONED BASE/GUARD TOWER – DAY

Radek is sitting on the ground. Trembling.

Dr Ventress sits on a chair, on the far side of the room, observing Radek with a neutral expression.

Lena and Thorensen are standing.

> RADEK
> We have to go back. We have to go back now.

> THORENSEN
> She's right.

> DR VENTRESS
> Right in what sense?

> THORENSEN
> We've been attacked twice, we've lost one of the team, and we have evidence that the previous team went nuts and chopped each other up. How more 'right' could she be?

> DR VENTRESS
> We haven't reached the lighthouse. We still don't understand the cause or nature of the Shimmer.

> THORENSEN
> We have data, observations, photographs, samples –

> DR VENTRESS
> – all of which make the phenomenon less explicable, not more.

She stands and walks to the door.

> I'm going to get to the lighthouse. I'll do it alone, if need be. You only need to decide whether you're coming with me, or not.

She exits.

Leaving Lena, Thorensen and Radek.

Silence.

> RADEK

It's like she hasn't even noticed that Sheppard is dead.

> THORENSEN

. . . She's crazy. A crazy old bitch.

Then Thorensen turns to Lena.

And thanks for the fucking back-up.

> LENA

I didn't know there were sides.

> THORENSEN

There are sides.

Lena hesitates.

> LENA

Okay. Then I agree with you. We should be heading back.

Thorensen looks relieved.

> THORENSEN

Right. Right! Good. The three of us can –

> LENA
> (*interrupts*)

Hold on a minute. We head back: yes. But not by retracing the route we took here. We don't know how many days it took us to reach this point, right? But we do know the ocean is two days away. And as Sheppard said: once we hit the shore, we can follow it until we hit the perimeter wall. It's impossible to get lost on the coast, and it will be easier terrain than the swamps.

> THORENSEN

You're saying we get out by going deeper in?

> LENA

If you like, yes.

THORENSEN

If I 'like'? No, Lena, I don't fucking 'like'.

Thorensen doesn't disguise her suspicion.

This isn't just a way of talking us round so we keep heading for the lighthouse?

LENA

It has nothing to do with the lighthouse. I believe the coast is the best route out. That's all.

Thorensen glances at Radek.

The younger woman has closed her eyes. Just trying to block it all out.

THORENSEN
(*under her breath*)

Shit.

INT. INTERROGRATION ROOM – DAY

Lomax.

LOMAX

You lied to them.

LENA

I didn't know what turning back meant. Who was to say it was safer than moving forwards?

LOMAX

Yes. You didn't know. But you made a decision to continue as if you did.

LENA

Ventress made the decision.

LOMAX

But Ventress was never coming back.

LENA

What do you mean?

                    LOMAX
She was sick.

                    LENA
. . . Cancer.

                    LOMAX
Yes.

Beat.

                    LENA
Of course. All damaged goods here.

Cut to:

EXT. SWAMP – DAY

The four-person team walk in single file.

Dr Ventress on point. Then Radek. Then Thorensen. Then Lena.

As they walk, Lena becomes aware that Thorensen is talking to herself.

Low muttering. Unintelligible. Some kind of internal private argument, unwittingly externalised.

Lena watches.

                    LENA
Hey.

Thorensen's gaze flicks round.

There's a flash of something in her eyes.

Something like anger. Something like a lack of recognition. A glassy stare, as if whatever she's seeing at that moment, it isn't Lena.

Then it's gone.

                    THORENSEN
What?

                              LENA
     You okay?

Thorensen turns away.

                           THORENSEN
     I'm fine. Leave me the fuck alone.

Cut to:

Dr Ventress, stopping.

She's seen something just ahead.

*Reveal crushed undergrowth, forming a trail into the trees. And
along it, unmistakable splashes and smears of blood on the
leaves.*

The others reach her.

                              RADEK
     . . . Sheppard.

                              LENA
     She might still be alive.

                          DR VENTRESS
     That seems unlikely.

                              LENA
     We need to know.

                          DR VENTRESS
     Go.

Beat.

                              LENA
     Fine.

Lena cocks her rifle.

                           THORENSEN
     I'll come with you.

Lena glances at Thorensen.

*Again, sees something in her eyes. A sheen or glaze. Something
not right.*

LENA

I'll go alone. Quicker, quieter.

EXT. SWAMP – DAY

Lena heads through the swamp.

Gun raised. Following the blood trail.

From somewhere nearby, she hears a noise.

Perhaps the bear. Perhaps something else.

She freezes.

Looks into the trees.

There is movement in the foliage. Something could be out there – a creature, or person. Or equally it could be a trick of the light, and shadows.

Lena watches. Waits.

Sees something.

But it's not the bear.

It's a deer.

Or a deer-like creature.

Elongated legs. Branch and leaf structures flowing out of its back.

Then – skittish – it's gone.

Sweat runs down Lena's face. She blinks it out of her eyes.

Silence returns.

Lena heads on.

EXT. SWAMP/CLEARING – DAY

Dense foliage.

In it, we find Lena.

Crawling forwards on her belly.

She's seen something up ahead.

Reveal –

– the end of the blood trail, in a clearing.

In the middle of the clearing, sunlit, is Sheppard. Lying on her back, facing upwards.

Lena watches.

Waits.

No sound, except wind in trees.

EXT. SWAMP/CLEARING – DAY

Lena cautiously approaches Sheppard's body, gun raised, continually scanning the treeline.

As she reaches her colleague –

– reveal Sheppard.

She has been pulled through undergrowth. There is some tearing on her clothes, and plant-matter in her hair. Dry blood on her skin.

And although her torso is badly damaged, bitten and clawed, and one of her ankles is clearly broken, her face is relatively untouched.

In fact, her expression seems peaceful. Her open eyes make her look as if she is gazing at the sunlight that filters through the canopy above.

Then –

– something strange happens.

Sheppard's left eye – and her left eye only – makes a sudden jittering movement. Like a quiver.

Lena jumps.

LENA
                          LENA
    Jesus!

*Then Sheppard's slightly parted lips move. As if just starting to
form a word.*

                          LENA
   . . . Sheppard?

Cut back to Sheppard's face –

*– as Sheppard's mouth is pushed more fully open, which reveals
that inside her mouth, there is a creature.*

*It is a microscopic creature – a tardigrade – but it has grown to
the size a large beetle.*

*Sheppard's mouth is full of them. They are feeding off the soft
matter of her tongue.*

*Sheppard's cheeks undulate gently with the movement, and the
left eye suddenly starts to sink into the socket, as it is consumed.*

Cut to:

EXT. SWAMP – DAY

*Lena, returning to where Dr Ventress, Thorensen and Radek
are waiting.*

                          RADEK
   Did you find her?

                          LENA
   She's dead.

The finality in Lena's voice dissuades follow-up questions.

*Wordlessly, Radek, Thorensen and Dr Ventress shoulder their
backpacks.*

EXT. SWAMP – DAY

Distant from the small group.

They are far figures, moving through the green.

Flitting in and out of view.

Then merged totally. Gone.

EXT. THE SUN – SUNDOWN

The light of the setting sun, refracting into a rainbow.

EXT. OUTSIDE VILLE PERDU – SUNDOWN

The four women stand on a dirt road.

Ahead is a small town. A backwater place. The buildings are largely single-storey. Abandoned vehicles have rusted, their tyres deflated.

And a dense kudzu-like plant-life has been busy reclaiming all the structures.

The moss tumour-growths are even more extreme here. Some of the buildings are half swallowed by the red and green clusters.

> DR VENTRESS
> This is where we camp tonight. The ocean is another two hours' hike from here. We pick a building. Secure the windows and doors. And we don't venture out until sun-up.

EXT. VILLE PERDU – SUNDOWN

The women enter the town.

Not talking.

Scanning. Alert.

Weapons unslung, and hands resting with the finger above the trigger guard.

Lena is distracted by the sight of one of the houses – from which a tree has appeared to grow from the inside. Branches push out through the windows and roof shingles.

Lena.

The quiet urgency in Radek's voice makes everyone look round.

Radek is frozen to the spot.

Lena follows her gaze –

– and jolts.

In the junction of the street ahead, there is what appears to be the silhouette of a man.

Motionless. Arms at his side. Facing them.

Thorensen whips her gun up to her shoulder.

There is something strange about the man.

He's slightly misshapen. His arms and torso are too thin. His legs are too thick.

Moreover, he hasn't moved.

Lena takes a step towards the man. Raises a hand.

LENA

Hello?

The silhouette of the man doesn't react at all.

Lena takes another step –

– and the shift in perspective reveals another figure.

This one is behind the man, behind the building. Not in shadow, but caught in the light from the dropping sun.

It looks like a child.

Also motionless, also misshapen.

But now, in the light, the oddness of the shape makes more sense.

The child is not flesh and blood, but plant. A twisting root system form calves and feet, leading up to knotted branches and densely packed leaves.

Like a topiary.

EXT. VILLE PERDU/STATUE AREA – SUNDOWN

Lena, followed by the others, walks through the space between the buildings, past the shape of the man –

– into a street that is something like a statue garden.

Dotted around the area, by the rusted shapes of abandoned cars, on plant-choked sidewalks and front lawns –

– there are twenty or so plant figures.

Seen from the correct angle, they appear as close facsimiles of a man, or woman, or a child.

From the wrong angle, they are a shapeless mass of plant form, or incomplete forms. The legs, and half the torso, an outstretched arm, becoming a tangle of twigs and leaves beyond the bicep.

Others have exploded far beyond the basic outline of a human, expanding out into tree structures.

> THORENSEN
>
> What are these things? Were they made by the people who lived here? Or one of the previous teams?

Lena examines a child plant.

> LENA
>
> I don't think they were made by anyone.

Lena plucks a leaf from the child figure.

> They've grown this way.

> THORENSEN
>
> What are you talking about? That makes no sense.

Radek speaks quietly.

> RADEK
>
> I think it does.

All turn to Radek.

Radek walks to one of the figures.

I'd thought the radio-waves were blocked by the Shimmer, and that's why no one inside could communicate with base or GPS. But look up. See the clouds. The sky.

Bright rainbow colours fringe the clouds above.

The light waves aren't blocked. They're refracted.

Radek reaches for her short-wave radio, hooked on her belt, and switches it on.

And it's the same with the radios. The signals aren't gone –

Through the static fuzz, there are sounds. Pulses. Soft distorted tones, that rise and fall.

– they're scrambled.

Radek switches the radio off.

Shifts her gaze to Lena.

The leaf in your hand. Do you know what you'd find if you sequenced it? Human hox genes.

THORENSEN
Hox? What are you talking about?

LENA
They're the genes that define body plan. The physical structure.

RADEK
And the plants have human body plan. Arms are attached to shoulders. Legs to hips.

Lena is trying to collect her thoughts, mind racing.

LENA
It's literally not possible.

RADEK
It's literally what's happening. The Shimmer is a prism, but it refracts everything. Not just light and radio waves. Animal DNA, plant DNA . . .

99

Radek hesitates.

> . . . All DNA.

Thorensen interrupts, overwhelmed by confusion and frustration.

> THORENSEN
> What do you mean, 'all DNA'?

> DR VENTRESS
> She means our DNA.

Lena lets her hand drop.

> She means us.

In the low sun, everything upright is silhouette, fringed with gold.

On the ground, the long shadows of the women and the plant statues are fringed with chromatic aberration, indistinguishable from each other.

EXT. VILLE PERDU/HOUSE – TWILIGHT

The women are outside the front entrance of a small house – a compact two-storey building.

The building had been boarded up before the town was evacuated.

Lena and Dr Ventress force open the front doors.

INT. VILLE PERDU/HOUSE/FRONT ROOM – NIGHT

The women set up camp inside the front room.

In the layout of its rooms, the house is an exact echo of Lena's home – a front hall with a staircase, a front room off the hall, and a kitchen at the back.

But this space is heavily decayed, and leaves little indication of the kind of home it once was, or the people who lived there.

Lena, Dr Ventress and Radek illuminate the area with their flashlights and work-lamps.

Thorensen keeps to herself.

She's sitting on her bedding. Lost slightly to her surroundings. Unnaturally focused.

Talking very quietly to herself. Staring with strange intensity at her hands. At the tips of her fingers.

EXT. THE MOON – NIGHT

The moon in the sky, through the Shimmer.

INT. VILLE PERDU/HOUSE/FRONT ROOM – NIGHT

Dr Ventress, Thorensen and Radek lie on their bedding.

Lena is watching them. Their soft breathing.

Satisfying herself that they're all asleep.

INT. VILLE PERDU/HOUSE/KITCHEN – NIGHT

Lena sits in the kitchen, at the dining table. Her work-lamp lights up the space.

From her backpack, she removes a small case: her research kit – field microscope, sample vials, and a scalpel.

She removes a sterile blade from a sealed foil packet.

Clips a blade into the scalpel.

Then she rolls up her left shirt sleeve.

It reveals her forearm –

– and the unexplained bruise she first noticed while talking to Sheppard as they paddled through the swamp.

The mark is now darker. And larger. Roughly circular, with a slight indication of a pattern. It's as if the bruise were painted with ink on wet paper, and the marks have blurred into something too abstract to understand.

Lena gazes at the strange, oddly malign shape.

Then pricks the scalpel into it. Drawing blood from the dark marks.

Extreme close-up on the crimson bead.

Cut to:

Lena leaning over her microscope.

Cut to:

Extreme close-up on blood cells. The biconcave shape is clearly visible.

The magnification increases. We see inside the translucent cell structure –

– where something is shimmering.

Cut to:

Lena, leaning away from the microscope.

Blank-faced.

Then she stands.

Goes directly to the kitchen sink.

And – quietly, with a minimum of fuss – throws up.

Cut to:

EXT. SKY – DAY

Close-up on the moon in daylight.

Cut to:

INT. JOHNS HOPKINS MEDICAL SCHOOL/SEMINAR ROOM – DAY

Lena, talking to her students in her seminar room.

> LENA
> So we can describe cancer as a mutation that causes
> unregulated cell growth. But mutation is also the reason

we exist. Without it, we wouldn't have evolved from the single-cell organism from which we're all derived.

She pauses.

I think it's partly why we find cancer so disturbing. It doesn't just hurt us and kill us, like a bullet, or the impact of a car crash. It changes us.

Cut to:

EXT. VILLE PERDU/STATUE AREA – NIGHT

The moonlit human plant-shapes.

Not quite motionless. Moving gently in wind.

Cut to:

INT. HOUSE/BEDROOM – NIGHT

Lena's face, moonlit.

Seen over a man's shoulder.

In bed. Having sex.

Cut to:

INT. HOUSE/BEDROOM – NIGHT

Lena.

Now sitting at her bedroom window. Gazing out at the night sky over the suburban street.

Reveal the man on the bed behind her.

It isn't Kane.

It's her work colleague. Daniel.

Beats pass.

Then Lena speaks.

This was a mistake.

DANIEL

Okay . . .

He pauses.

But it's a mistake we keep making. It's not exactly the first time I've been in your bed, or you in mine. Whenever he goes away, we find ourselves right here.

LENA

It's still a mistake.

Daniel half laughs.

DANIEL

You want to have this conversation again?

Silence.

Fine. Let's have it again. You spend more time away from your husband than with him. You can't talk to him about your work, and he won't talk to you about his. And there is a clear physical and intellectual connection between us. Have I covered the bases?

LENA

You didn't mention your wife.

DANIEL

I love my wife, as I always make plain. She's blameless in this.

He sits up in bed.

Come on, Lena. What's really going on here?

Lena doesn't answer. She's zoned him out.

Is it because you haven't heard from him? You think . . .

He hesitates.

. . . You think something may have happened to him?

Beat.

Or you think he knows. That's it, isn't it? You think
somehow he's found out about our affair.

*The note of anxiety in Daniel's voice pulls Lena out of her glaze.
He's clearly more worried by the idea that Kane knows about
their affair than Kane being KIA.*

. . . Has he found out?

Lena glances back at Daniel.

Watches him for a moment.

Flat. Dead.

LENA

You should go.

Daniel frowns.

DANIEL

Look, Lena, I –

LENA

Dan.

Daniel cuts himself off.

I'm not interested in talking to you, or anything you have
to say. Just get dressed and get out.

A beat.

Then Daniel stands.

Starts to put on his clothes.

DANIEL
You know it's not me you hate. It's yourself.

LENA
No, Dan. It's you too.

Lena turns away, back to the window.

Close on Lena's face.

> This is never going to happen again.

She shuts her eyes.

Behind her, out of sight, we hear Daniel leave.

Then –

– we hear Thorensen's voice.

THORENSEN
(*out of shot*)

> You lying bitch.

The voice intrudes in the way an alarm clock intrudes on a dream. The sudden awareness that the alarm is real, and the dream is not.

Cut to:

INT. VILLE PERDU/HOUSE/FRONT ROOM – NIGHT

Lena opening her eyes.

And seeing Thorensen.

Standing over her. Holding her automatic rifle. Watching Lena with her glassy stare.

LENA

> . . . What's going on?

Thorensen shakes her head.

THORENSEN

> No.

Everything about Thorensen now has the LSD off-rhythm of someone not sharing the same reality as those around them.

> You don't ask that question. You answer it.

At that, Thorensen spins her rifle around, and smashes the stock down. Knocking Lena out cold.

Cut to black.

Then:

INT. VILLE PERDU/HOUSE/FRONT ROOM – NIGHT

Lena coming round. Groggy. Nauseous.

Finding she is gagged, and sitting on a kitchen chair. Forearms tied to the chair itself, behind her back. Blood running down her face from a cut inside her hairline.

Radek and Dr Ventress are beside her, also on kitchen chairs, and similarly bound.

Their backs are to the hallway.

And Thorensen is in front of them.

Standing. Facing away. Shoulders shaking.

It takes Lena a moment to realise that Thorensen is crying.

The strangeness of the moment extends.

Lena pulls at her wrists. Exchanges a glance with Dr Ventress.

Thorensen wipes her eyes.

Then turns.

Faces Lena.

We can immediately see: Thorensen is not at the edge of sanity. She's tipped past it.

She lifts a hand.

A silver chain is dangling from her fingers.

An open locket. Inside, the photo of Kane.

Horror in Lena's eyes. A sharp suck of air through her nose.

THORENSEN
Boyfriend. Brother. Husband.

Thorensen sees something in Lena's expression.

Husband.

Beat.

Why didn't you tell us?

Lena tries to speak through her gag.

Thorensen observes blankly.

Then her eyes flick to Dr Ventress.

You knew. Obviously.

Dr Ventress meets the gaze. Gives nothing.

Thorensen looks to Radek.

How about you?

Radek shakes her head.

Thorensen nods.

Takes a moment.

There were the two theories about what went wrong in the Shimmer. One, something in here killed them. Two, they went crazy and killed each other.

Beat.

Josie nearly got killed by a gator. Cass did get killed by a bear. So okay, yes, theory one. It fits.

Beat.

But . . .

A tear spills down Thorensen's face. The composure is suddenly cracking again.

. . . I didn't actually see a bear. And Josie didn't see a bear. The only people who saw a bear were Lena and Ventress. And Lena didn't want me to see Cass's body, so nothing is confirmed. Everything is on their word. On Lena's word.

Thorensen looks at the locket in her hand.

And what we know now . . . What we know . . .

She glances at Lena.

. . . is that Lena is a liar.

Beat.

Did you kill Cass?

Lena's eyes widen. She starts shaking her head.

Was it because she was going to turn back? Did you lose
your shit? Or do you think I've lost my shit? And now
we're going to fuck each other up. It's theory two.

Beat.

When I look at my hands, my fingerprints, I feel I can see
them move. I mean, I can't actually see them move, but
moment by moment, they aren't the same.

She gives a little sob.

If I let you go, and you tie me to the chair, and you cut me
open, will my insides will be moving like my fingerprints?
That fucking scares me.

She recomposes. Takes a breath.

But I'm not tied to the chair. You are.

Beat.

We really got to establish . . .

Thorensen reaches down her belt. And unclips her knife.

Is it theory one? Is it theory two?

Lena and Dr Ventress desperately try to talk through their gags.

Thorensen ignores them.

*They struggle against their bonds as she approaches, holding the
knife in her hands.*

And just as she reaches them –

– there is the sound of a scream.

It's a woman. But it's not inside the room. It's from somewhere outside.

And we've heard it before. It's the sound Sheppard made as she was being killed in the forest.

The screams fade out.

A beat of stunned silence in the room.

Broken by Thorensen.

    Cass?

Another sudden intense burst of screaming.

And it sounds closer. And within it, we can hear words.

                SHEPPARD
                (*out of shot*)
Help me – oh God please – please help me –

It cuts out again.

                THORENSEN
    Oh Jesus – it is Cass.

To Lena.

    You said she was fucking dead. You said you saw her!

Bang.

All jump.

Something has knocked against the front of the house.

All heads turn to the sound of the noise.

                SHEPPARD
                (*out of shot*)
    Please – please –

Sheppard's voice is now right outside the vine-choked window.

Something scratches against the wood.

                              SHEPPARD
                              (*out of shot*)
            Oh God, I'm hurt –

                              THORENSEN
            Oh fuck.

Thorensen exits the front room into the hallway, heading for the front door.

With Thorensen now out of the room, Lena immediately starts to struggle against her bindings.

                              SHEPPARD
                              (*out of shot*)
            I'm bleeding –

                              THORENSEN
            Hold on –

                              SHEPPARD
                              (*out of shot*)
            Hurry –

We hear the door pull open.

                              THORENSEN
            . . . Cass? Are you –

The sentence suddenly cuts out. Thorensen makes a single sound, short, curtailed – like a sudden constriction in her neck.

Silence.

Lena and Ventress exchange a glance.

Then there is a sound from the hallway.

Scraping again. Something sharp and heavy. Pulled on the floorboards.

Then an animal breathing.

Then Sheppard's voice, one last time.

                              SHEPPARD
            Help me.

Because their backs are to the hallway, the women have to crane their heads around to see what's coming.

Moments later it appears around the entrance to the hall.

It's not Sheppard.

It's the bear-like creature that killed her.

Mutated jaw. Hairless, strangely pigmented skin. Lesions.

Elongated claws – the cause of the scraping noise as it moves.

Eyes reflecting light from the room as bright yellow discs.

The Bear turns to look at them.

A beat on the strange scene: the three women tied to chairs, the freakish creature.

Then the Bear opens its jaws, and a human-like noise emerges. A thin sigh, as if we are hearing Sheppard's final breaths . . .

. . . and starts to move again.

Into the room.

Instinctively, they turn away, as if by avoiding eye-contact with the creature it might ignore them.

But it doesn't. Moments later, its huge head and shoulders appears directly behind them.

Sniffing at them. Breathing into their hair.

Its mutated snout nuzzles Lena. Pushing up against her cheek.

Lena's fists tighten, controlling her fear, controlling her breathing. Just.

Then it moves on. Up behind Radek.

It pushes its snout against the back of her head. Radek fails to control her panic. There is a high whimper in her breathing.

The Bear reacts. Hearing. And now finding extra interest in Radek.

A beat.

Then it starts to move again.

Around from the back of the three women . . .

. . . to the front.

Now appearing right in their line of sight. Unavoidable. Colossal.

It moves past Dr Ventress.

Then moves past Lena.

Then stops at Radek.

Radek's eyes are tight closed. Terrified.

A beat. Then she opens them.

And sees the creature's face. Directly in front of hers.

The jaws open, the creature pushes in . . .

. . . and slowly bites into Radek's shoulder.

Radek gasps.

LENA
(*whispers, urgent*)

Don't move. Don't react.

The bite is slow. And stops. It's not tearing into Radek. It's compressing. Testing.

Blood starts to run into the material of Radek's shirt.

The bite compresses harder.

Radek can't stand it any more.

She screams.

The creature immediately reacts.

Releases Radek – only to open its jaw wide. Then it roars, and twists its head, to strike.

At that moment –

– reveal in the entrance way to the hall:

113

Thorensen.

She's badly wounded, chest soaked in blood from something that happened to her neck.

But she's upright, and holding her rifle, aimed at the Bear.

And as the Bear rears up – she shoots.

Hits the Bear in the shoulder.

The Bear reacts. Head snaps to Thorensen.

Then it suddenly charges – directly through the three women tied to chairs.

They are knocked across the room with immense force.

Radek's chair breaks as they land, freeing her arms.

The Bear slams into Thorensen, knocking her into the hallway wall.

Lena is sideways on the ground, still bound. She starts to kick herself back against the wall, with as much violence as possible, to smash the chair that still holds her.

Radek pulls the ropes off, and crawls across the floor to her rifle.

Thorensen tries to pull herself up the hall stairs. The Bear bites into her leg. Pulls her back with massive force – yanking out the banisters that Thorensen attempts to cling to. At the bottom of the stairs, the Bear rips into Thorensen with its jaws around her neck, and kills her.

Lena has kicked herself free, just as the Bear re-enters the front room.

The Bear charges Lena, jamming her backwards into the corner of the room.

Lena is pressed back against the floor and wall, with the Bear above and over her. Its blood-smeared jaws open, preparing to kill her in the same way it just killed Thorensen.

Then, inexplicably, the head starts to blow apart. Chunks, strands of flesh, blood vapour – pulling themselves off the Bear's deformed head –

– before we, and Lena, can make sense of it. And we start to hear through the crescendo of noise – the score, the roaring – the sound of gunfire.

And reveal Radek. Holding her rifle. Emptying it.

For a final moment the Bear and its shattered skull remain upright.

Then it falls.

Cut to:

EXT. VILLE PERDU/STATUE GARDEN – NIGHT

The sculpture garden in moonlight.

On one of the figures, a flower is drawing open, like a daisy unfurling in sunlight.

Cut to:

INT. VILLE PERDU/HOUSE/FRONT ROOM – NIGHT

Lena covering Thorensen's body with one of the rain ponchos.

Radek watches Lena. Catches her eye as she turns.

Cut to:

Dr Ventress, packing hurriedly. Jamming kit into her backpack.

                    LENA
. . . What are you doing?

                    DR VENTRESS
Leaving.

                    LENA
Now?

DR VENTRESS

We're an hour from the coast. The road will take me straight there. I don't expect you to come with me.

LENA

It's not even light.

DR VENTRESS

I don't have time to wait. We're disintegrating! Our minds as fast as our bodies. Can't you feel it?

Dr Ventress shoulders the pack. Picks up her gun.

It's like the onset of dementia. If I don't reach the lighthouse soon, the person that started the journey won't be the person that ends it.

At the door, Dr Ventress looks back at Lena and Radek.

I want to be the one that ends it.

Then Dr Ventress exits. Into the night.

EXT. VILLE PERDU – SUNRISE

First light, over the town.

EXT. VILLE PERDU/STATUE AREA – SUNRISE

Radek stands among the statues.

Many of the plant figures are now dotted with small white flowers.

A few beats of quiet.

Then Lena appears nearby, carrying her gun and backpack.

LENA

Josie. We should go.

Radek doesn't move.

RADEK

How long was your husband in the Shimmer?

LENA

. . . I don't know. It's hard to be sure. Theoretically, as long
as a year.

RADEK

As long as a year . . .

Beat.

Amazing to have been inside so long, and remained intact.

LENA

. . . I don't think he was intact, Josie.

RADEK

No. I suppose not.

Silence.

I'm right about the refractions, aren't I?

LENA

Yes. I tested my blood last night. It's in me.

Radek nods.

RADEK

It will be in all of us.

Radek starts walking through the figures.

It was so strange, hearing Sheppard's voice in the mouth
of that creature last night. I think as she was dying, part of
her mind became part of the creature that was killing her.

Lena loses sight of Radek for a moment.

Can still hear her.

Imagine. Dying frightened and in pain, and having that as
the only part of you which survives. Trapped in an animal.

Lena steps into the figures.

Trying to catch sight of Radek.

Then spots her – a little distance away. Framed between two of

*the green humanoids. Not quite in the area we would have
expected to see her, in relation to her previous position.*

I wouldn't like that at all.

Radek looks down at her arm.

But the problem isn't just what part of us gets trapped in
something else.

*Close-up on Radek's arm, as she runs her thumb over the pale
self-harm scars on her forearms.*

When she pulls her thumb away –

– something moves in her flesh.

Not just a flex. Much more fundamental.

A bone, shifting and contracting.

Or a muscle, worming its way to a new position.

It's what part of something else gets trapped in us.

Radek looks back at Lena. Through the green figures.

Ventress wants to face it.

Radek moves again.

You want to fight it.

Lena loses sight again.

Hears Radek.

But I don't think I want either of those things.

Lena steps forwards.

LENA

Josie.

No answer.

Lena moves more quickly.

She's reached the point where Radek was just standing.

Lena stops. Scans. Can't see her.

Lena calls out.

> Josie!

The answering silence is far too absolute.

A sudden pulse of panic in Lena.

A sudden knowledge: somehow, Radek is gone.

She stares at the figures around her. Checking them, as if one of them might be Radek.

Runs deeper into the statue garden. Surrounded by the mute forms.

LENA

> JOSIE!

Again. More frantic

> JOSIE!

Nothing.

Radek has vanished. Into the trees, or into the humanoid forms.

Lena is alone.

Cut to:

INT. INTERROGATION ROOM

Lomax and Lena.

LOMAX
One by one. All gone. Except you.

Beat.

How do you explain that?

Lena frowns.

LENA
Is it something I need to explain?

> LOMAX
> (*flat*)
> Yes. You do.

Beat.

Lena considers, as if for the first time.

Then:

> LENA
> I wanted to come back. More than anything. I had to come back.

Beat.

> LENA
> I'm not sure any of them did.

Cut to:

PART THREE – TO THE LIGHTHOUSE

Cut to:

EXT. FOREST PATH – DAY

Lena walking alone down a forest path.

Ahead, through the trees, we can glimpse dunes and the ocean.

Stretching across the path are bands of colour that appear to be flowers –

– until Lena passes through the bands of colour, and the flowers near her suddenly scatter, and lift into the air.

And we realise they are butterflies.

EXT. BEACH – DAY

A long hook of beach, where the swamp gives way to the sea.

Massively empty. Miles of undulating dunes, and the great flat ocean.

Along the beach, strange shapes rise.

Visually similar to the tumour-like growths on the plants and buildings –

– but these are made of sand. Like massive termite mounds, as much as thirty foot high, morphed into spires and oddly organic abstractions.

Only one other landmark can be seen.

A couple of miles distant, seen through a blue haze of air and sea spray.

The lighthouse.

Slender, tall. And white – where one can still see of the original construction, behind the brightly coloured moss.

Leading that direction, a snaking line of footprints are clearly visible in the damp sand.

The trail left by Dr Ventress.

Cut to:

Lena.

Standing on the pale sands.

Wind pulls at her hair.

She slips off her backpack.

She looks down at her arm –

– where the bruise has now resolved into something immediately recognisable.

The dark circle and blurred indication of patterns have become a tattoo.

Exactly the same distinctive image that Thorensen wore.

The ouroboros.

EXT. THE OCEAN – DAY

From the ocean, a single figure walks along the shore.

Between the abstract sand structures.

In the foreground, a huge whale-like creature breaches the surface –

– then slides back beneath the waves.

EXT. BEACH/LIGHTHOUSE – DAY

Lena stands on the beach.

The lighthouse is still a few metres away.

The area here is littered with bones and scraps of clothing.

The scene of a massacre, many years ago.

Blown and blasted by the wind, sand, sun, and salt.

The bones look like ivory. A bright red backpack has been bleached pink. The body beneath it has almost been completely submerged into the dune.

Lena reaches down and picks up the top half of a skull.

The back of the skull morphs into the star-shape of a vertebrae, as if it had been fused with its own backbone.

Lena drops it back on the sand.

Then continues towards the tall, white lighthouse building.

EXT. LIGHTHOUSE – DAY

Lena approaches the lighthouse.

Tumour-forms cover almost the entire structure.

Below, at its base, its door hangs open, swinging in the sea breeze, knocking gently against its frame.

INT. LIGHTHOUSE – DAY

Lena enters the base of the lighthouse.

Light filters down from the window, thirty metres above, illuminating the room.

The interior walls are covered in the same tumour-growths as the exterior.

A staircase winds up the circular wall to the top of the structure.

Abandoned on the floor, there is some military gear. A backpack, surrounded by cannister-shaped grenades, and a rifle.

Opposite where Lena enters, there is a tunnel in the floor, about two metres in diameter. At its entrance, the wooden boards have been pulled up, and laid out as a kind of ramp structure, leading downwards.

Inside the tunnel something glows. The soft, blue-green light of phosphorescence.

Finally, in the middle of the room there is a video camera on a tripod. The camera faces a long black scorch mark, rising up the curved wall, from a blackened heap on the ground. The nature of the heap is unclear. It's charred and fused beyond all recognition.

Lena takes this all in.

Her gaze finally settling on the camera.

Cut to:

INT. LIGHTHOUSE – NIGHT

Playback on the camera.

The position is locked off, on a tripod, in the middle of the room.

It faces Kane.

Kane is sitting on the floor, cross-legged, with his back to the curved wall.

Holding something in his hands.

                    KANE
    I thought I was a man.

He pauses.

I had a life. People called me Kane. But now I'm not sure.

Beat.

If I wasn't Kane, what was I?

He looks at the Cameraman.

Was I you? Were you me?

The Cameraman doesn't answer.

My flesh moves like liquid. My mind is cut loose.

Beat.

Then Kane looks straight down the lens.

His pupils glow like cat's eyes in the infra-red light.

I can't bear it.

He opens his palm.

He's holding one of the canister-shaped grenades.

He glances up at the Cameraman.

Ever see a phosphorus grenade go off? Shield your eyes.
They're kind of bright.

He hesitates.

If you ever get back, find Lena.

CAMERAMAN
I will.

Kane pulls the pin on the grenade.

There is a soft quick ticking, like a wristwatch by your ear.

Kane gazes directly at the camera. Unafraid.

KANE
Five, four, three, two –

The grenade detonates.

A blinding white flame, as if Kane is suddenly holding the sun in his lap. A high-pressure rush of noise.

Initially, we can scarcely see Kane's shape through the glow.

Then it dims slightly, starting to burn itself out.

We see his blackened shape bend. Fall forwards on to the sun.

A couple of moments pass.

The flare continues to die down.

Then –

– the Cameraman walks forward. Stepping into frame.

It's our first ever view of him.

His back is to us.

He gazes at the hunched charcoal figure, as it continues to blaze with the fierce white light.

Then he turns his head. And in the etched light of the phosphorus, we see his face.

It's Kane. Clean-shaven – as we first saw him, when he appeared at Lena's house.

On this –

– the image freezes.

Cut to:

INT. LIGHTHOUSE – DAY

Lena.

Staring at the small screen on the camera, which remains frozen on Kane's face.

LENA
(whispers)

No.

Her eyes flick to the blackened heap under the scorch marks.

Now able to make sense of the shape.

No, no, no . . .

She is interrupted by a sound.

A distorted scream. Echoed and distant, as if having passed through passages and chambers.

Female.

Dr Ventress.

It's coming from the torn up floorboards. The tunnel, that leads down into bedrock.

Lena looks to where the floorboards have been pulled up.

To the tunnel entrance, and the soft blue-green light.

Lena controls her fear.

Knuckles white around the grip of her rifle.

INT. UNDER THE LIGHTHOUSE/TUNNEL – CONTINUOUS

Lena makes her way down the tunnel, gun raised.

The walls continue the curve of the lighthouse above, and the floor is sloping downwards –

– which means the passage is corkscrewing into the ground.

It is unclear how the rock has been cleared. The walls, ceiling, and floor are made of smooth black rock, like obsidian.

The rock is rippled, as if worn smooth by an ancient stream or lava flow.

It is seamed with phosphorescence – illuminating everything in the way that sea creatures light their way in the depths.

And the walls seem to be moving.

Or gently undulating.

The surfaces of the walls are covered in cilia. Tiny anemone arms waving, caught in the flow of slow-moving water.

The flow movement is down. Deeper into the tunnel. As if what lies inside is feeding on what lies outside, and being channelled along a vein and capillary structure.

Then the tunnel stops, and opens out into a chamber.

INT. UNDER THE LIGHTHOUSE/CHAMBER – CONTINUOUS

The chamber is roughly semi-spherical. Three-quarters of a sphere, with the bottom levelled out into a floor.

The sculpted forms of humans and animals continue across the floor, but as they rise up the walls they taper into curved points.

Either side of these points, the walls are glassy smooth.

The arrangement is similar to petals, as if we are on the inside of a flower before it has unfurled. The interior of a vast lotus bulb.

The very centre of the chamber is particularly bright – because it is to here that the phosphorescent veins and channels all lead.

And standing on this brightest point –

– is Dr Ventress.

The doctor is internally lit. Cilia cover her skin like undulating fur. She shimmers gently.

Lena hesitates in the entrance.

Then takes a step inside the chamber.

Dr Ventress is talking to herself. Whispering. Barely audible. Abstract words.

DR VENTRESS
It's the last phase. Vanished into havoc. Unfathomable mind. Now beacon. Now sea.

Lena speaks.

LENA
Dr Ventress?

Dr Ventress breaks off.

Turns.

Sees Lena.

Then recognises her.

DR VENTRESS

. . . Lena.

Dr Ventress has the same expression as Kane when he appeared back home. Alzheimer's-like. In her eyes there is vagueness and confusion. And through the confusion, an unfocused sense of fear.

We spoke. What was it we said?

She pauses, remembering.

That I needed to know what was inside the lighthouse.

Dr Ventress looks at her glowing hands.

That moment's passed. It's inside me now.

LENA

. . . What's inside you?

DR VENTRESS

Something old. From far away.

The cilia on her palms move like wind over a wheat field.

It's not like us. It's unlike us. I don't know what it wants. Or if it wants.

As she talks, something disturbing begins to happen to Dr Ventress.

Splits, complex fissures, start rippling across her skin. As if her form is becoming unbalanced.

But it will grow until it encompasses everything. Our bodies and minds will be fragmented into their smallest parts. Until not one part remains.

She looks back at Lena.

Annihilation.

Then Dr Ventress can't speak any more.

She has started undergoing an extraordinary physical transformation.

It is a shape-shift of a kind that our mind cannot entirely make sense of – like an unfolding tesseract, unfolding and refolding from within itself, its interior indefinably becoming its exterior.

In this case, it is the doctor's skin that is unfolding and refolding.

Her face and body split into fractal twisting ribbons.

From out of the ribbons, radiating objects and energies emerge.

Ever-increasing size and complexity.

The concentric circles are endless.

The sense of expansion becomes vast.

Until the mesh of immense structural detail becomes –

– the mesh of undulating cilia on skin.

But Dr Ventress is gone.

Instead, we see fleeting glimpses of other bodies and faces.

Peyton, Mayer, and unknown team members from the previous expeditions.

Then for a moment it is Sheppard who stands in front of Lena. Her face splits open to reveal the head of the Bear.

Then it is Thorensen, with a the white intestine worm pushing out of her mouth.

Then it is Radek who stands in front of Lena. Her skin blossoming into small white flowers.

Then finally, the unfolding coalesces into a new shape.

Entirely non-human.

At this moment we are seeing the Alien. Its actual form. A Mandelbulb creature from the world of visualised mathematics. Infinitely complex, inexplicable in its movement.

Surrounded by radiating impressions of infinitely smaller versions of itself.

Lena and the Alien gaze at each other for a few hypnotic seconds.

Then the radiating shapes have filled the chamber.

They surround Lena.

Then Lena herself is starting to unfold. Unravel like fabric.

LENA

No –

Through this –

– she lifts her gun.

Like a dream –

– which shatters, the moment she squeezes the trigger and fires.

Bullets slam into the Alien.

Where they hit the body, a hole expands, like a bullet into ballistic gelatine – but does not contract.

Where they penetrate the body, they leave bright trails of light.

For a moment, the Alien is poised in this state.

Hugely misshapen.

Speared.

Then it expands.

Transforms.

And resolves –

– into a humanoid figure.

Sexless. Featureless. Having the arms, legs, head and torso of a human – man or woman. But nothing else.

No eyes, or mouth, or nose, or muscle form.

Lena is transfixed by the sight.

The figure turns to Lena.

And we see its smooth facial area. Internally lit. Cilia covering the skin like undulating fur, shimmering gently.

A beat, between the woman and the Humanoid.

Lena's weapon is out.

She has no more clips.

She starts to run.

The Humanoid observes her run.

Then it starts to follow her.

The first step is slow.

The second faster.

The third is as fluid and powerful as Lena.

It starts sprinting.

INT. UNDER THE LIGHTHOUSE/TUNNEL – CONTINUOUS

Lena climbs back up the tunnel.

Slips. Crashes to the ground.

Scrambles back up.

Cut to:

The Humanoid. In pursuit.

And we see something strange happen.

Where Lena fell and tripped –

– the Humanoid does exactly the same thing.

Falling in the same place. In the same way. An echo of Lena's action.

Cut to:

Lena, reaching the tunnel exit.

Climbing back up into the base of the lighthouse.

INT. LIGHTHOUSE – CONTINUOUS

Lena scrambles across the room –

– towards the door to the lighthouse.

But she doesn't make it.

The Humanoid simply appears in front of her, before she reaches the door.

It is unclear how it got there.

A frozen beat.

Then Lena strikes the Humanoid with all her strength.

And a moment later, in a mirror of her actions –

– the Humanoid strikes her back – but with incredible power.

Lena is sent flying backwards across the room.

She collides with the camera and tripod.

All skid across the room to the wall.

But it has provided Lena with a weapon. As the Humanoid reapproaches her, she picks up the tripod and swings it like a club, smashing the camera against the Humanoid's head.

And again, the Humanoid mirrors the actions. Using its arm like a club.

For a second time, Lena is sent hurtling back across the room by the force of the impact.

But this time towards Kane's backpack.

She collides with it, and the phosphorus grenades beside it.

And as she gets to her feet, the Humanoid is again on her.

Standing directly in front of her. Featureless, eyeless, but somehow watching.

Utterly, infinitely more powerful than she is.

For the first time, we see something beaten in Lena. Something broken.

LENA

Please –

She expects a killing blow.

And flinches –

– and the Humanoid does the same.

Lena sees.

She immediately realises what we already know. The Humanoid is mimicking her.

She is fighting herself.

We can see her thinking: can this be true?

The killing blow still hasn't come.

Lena lifts a hand.

Fingers trembling with adrenaline and fear.

And the Humanoid's opposite hand also rises.

She pauses.

The Humanoid's hand pauses.

Lena's hand starts moving again. Until –

– she touches its cheek.

An exact mirror of the gesture where she touched Kane's face at the start of the film, when he appeared at their bedroom at home.

A beat.

Then the Humanoid raises its hand.

Lena holds motionless, suspended, except for tight breathing and trickling beads of sweat, as the softly glowing hand lifts to her face . . .

Then –

– lightly touches her cheek also.

And as it does so –

– the Humanoid starts another folding transformation.

Rippling, folding, collapsing.

And this time, resolving itself –

– as Lena.

Lena gasps.

For a moment, the two face each other. Lena and her doppelgänger.

Reveal – at Lena's feet – the phosphorus grenades.

Close, on Lena. Processing. Controlling herself.

Then – slowly –

– she reaches down.

Opposite her, in a slightly delayed mirror action –

– her double does the same.

Lena's hand closes around one of the metal canisters.

Her double does the same.

Lena rises again. Never taking her eyes off her mirror-image face.

A final beat.

Lena watching Lena.

Then Lena pulls the pin.

The double mirrors.

Soft ticking from the canisters.

Seconds passing.

> LENA
> (*breathes*)
> Five, four, three, two –

Then –

Lena drops the grenade –

– and throws herself sideways.

The double is too late to fully react.

Lena's phosphorus grenade detonates.

And a moment later, so does the double's.

The interior of the lighthouse is suddenly illuminated by stark white light.

Lena scrambles for the exit –

– as behind her, we see the brightly burning form of the double.

Cut to:

EXT. LIGHTHOUSE – SUNDOWN

Lena escaping from the blaze, into the open air.

The sun is now setting.

The sand sculptures and tree line are lit like gold.

Cut to:

INT. LIGHTHOUSE – CONTINUOUS

Inside the lighthouse, the blazing figure reaches out a hand.

It touches the tumour-covered wall – which ignites at the point of contact. A burning handprint.

And a moment later, on the direct opposite side of the wall, the tumour ignites.

A mirror to the handprint.

The figure moves again, feeling its way around the circular wall.

Whatever it touches, ignites.

And opposite that ignition, a mirror ignition starts.

Looking top-down at the circular base of the lighthouse –

– a snowflake symmetry starts to emerge in the areas of ignition.

Where the alien has been absorbing, refracting, and mutating our plant, human, and animal DNA –

– it is now absorbing and mutating the intense fire of burning white phosphorus.

And these ignitions start to multiply themselves.

It is as if the white fire is metasticising.

And the figure becomes lost in the blaze, as the fire spreads up the interior walls of the lighthouse –

INT. UNDER THE LIGHTHOUSE/CHAMBER – CONTINUOUS

– and the walls of the chamber –

EXT. LIGHTHOUSE – CONTINUOUS

– and the exterior of the lighthouse.

Lena steps back, watching, as the entire lighthouse becomes consumed.

A huge tornado plume of unnatural flame.

Which blossoms out into a huge fireball, illuminating the entire landscape.

Casting long sundial shadows from the sand sculptures on the beach.

In the flames, a massive structure appears.

The form of the Alien that we glimpsed in the chamber, made now of billowing white fire.

It holds for a few seconds.

Then –

– the vast fireball starts to dissipate.

Literally burning itself out.

And as it does so –

– all along the beach, the sand sculptures start collapsing. First one, then three, then seven. Then all together.

Wind collects them as they fall.

Leaving one upright figure alone in the landscape.

Lena.

Cut to:

EXT. SOUTHERN REACH FACILITY/OBSERVATION AREA – SUNDOWN

The observation area of the Southern Reach Facility.

Where the Soldiers and Scientists of the Southern Reach gaze at the view over the scrubland to the treeline –

– where the Shimmer is now clearly melting away.

And the refractions are reverting to the blues, reds and oranges of a normal, beautiful sunset.

Then cut to:

EXT. THE NIGHT SKY – NIGHT

A star-field in a night sky.

Dense constellations. The Milky Way.

And the moon.

EXT. DEFORESTED AREA – DAY

A lone woman walks out of the treeline, and starts across the scrubland towards the Southern Reach facility.

Lena.

A few beats later, two vehicles appear, driving fast across the deforested area to intercept her.

Lena stops walking as they pull up.

Four Spec Ops Soldiers exit the vehicles and approach her.

Cut to:

INT. SOUTHERN REACH FACILITY/INTERVIEW ROOM – NIGHT

The interview room in which Lena was first interrogated by Dr Ventress.

And again, there is a Spec Ops soldier guarding the door.

But now, it's Lomax sitting opposite her.

And both he and the Spec Ops Guard are wearing a full biohazard suit.

There is a glass of water on the table in front of her.

                    LOMAX
    So. It was alien.

Beat.

    Can you describe its form?

The question hangs for a beat.

                    LENA
    No.

                    LOMAX
    Was it carbon-based?

                    LENA
    I don't know.

LOMAX

What did it want?

LENA

I don't think it wanted anything.

LOMAX

But it attacked you.

LENA

It mirrored me. I attacked it. I'm not sure it even knew I was there.

LOMAX

It came here for a reason. It was mutating our environment, it was destroying everything.

LENA

It wasn't destroying. It was changing everything. It was making something new.

LOMAX

Making what?

LENA

I don't know.

LOMAX

The team reached the lighthouse a few hours ago. Everything is ash. If what you encountered was once alive, it seems it's now dead.

Lena takes the glass of water.

LENA

Now will you tell me what happened to my husband?

Lena pauses.

LOMAX

When the Shimmer disappeared, his blood-pressure stabilised, and his pulse-rate started to rise. A few hours later, he was not only awake. He was lucid.

Beat.

He's still in isolation obviously.

                    LENA
So am I.

INT. SOUTHERN REACH FACILITY/WARD ROOM –
CONTINUOUS

*Kane sits in his quarantined ward room. In a chair. Gazing out
of the window at the night sky.*

A Nurse in a biohazard suit opens the door.

Lena enters.

Kane looks round, and they lock eyes.

Neither speak.

Then Lena closes the door behind her, making them alone.

Beat.

INT. OXYGEN TENT – DAY

Lena stares at Kane, uncertain.

Kane stands.

Takes a step towards her.

Then puts his arms around her –

– and they embrace. As they did at the start of the film.

*As they hold each other, we get two shots, close-ups on both
their eyes, which allows us to see the shimmer to each of them.*

                    LENA
You aren't Kane, are you?

Kane gives a slight shake of the head.

                    KANE
I don't think so.

Beat.

Are you Lena?

Lena hesitates, before turning to face him.

In the white of Kane's eye, we can see a rainbow sheen of refracted light. And deep in the dark pupils, a pulse of movement.

ANNIHILATION

Cut to:

EXT. LIGHTHOUSE – DAY

Wide on the burned structure of the lighthouse.

Traces of carbonised tumour still cling to the exterior.

Figures swarm around the base and beach. Soldiers and Scientists, photographing, taking samples, examining the skeletons on the beach, talking in groups.

Cut to:

The same view, but from high above, looking directly down.

The lighthouse is centred in the image.

And from this height, we can see something that was invisible at ground level – circular impressions in the landscape, ringing the lighthouse, defined by slight discolorations in the sand on the beach, and the green rushes that grow in the dunes.

The faint impressions radiate out in concentric rings.

Initially, it is like looking at the iris of an eye.

But as the camera drifts higher, and higher, we notice a familiar form start to resolve.

Now picked out in the bands of coloured foliage in the forest and swamps, the shadows of taller trees, the seabed beneath the waves, and the shape of the dunes themselves . . .

. . . The Alien.

A vast ghost form, imprinted in the living landscape.

BEHIND THE SCENES PHOTOS
BY MIYA MIZUNO

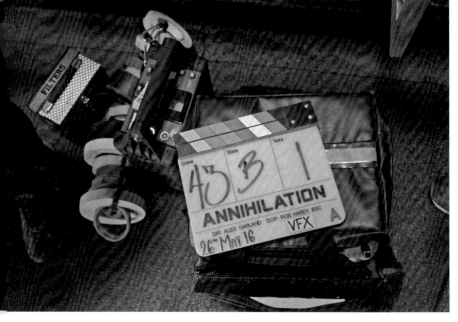